DISCIPLESHIP

IMPERFECT COVER

The *BEST* Writings
From the Most
Experienced
Disciple Makers

DISCIPLESHIP

Edited by
BILLIE HANKS, JR.,
and ## WILLIAM A. SHELL

ZONDERVAN
PUBLISHING HOUSE
OF THE ZONDERVAN CORPORATION
GRAND RAPIDS, MICHIGAN 49506

INTERNATIONAL
EVANGELICAL
ASSOCIATION

International Evangelism Association
Box 6883
Fort Worth, Texas 76115

Library of Congress Cataloging in Publication Data

Main entry under title:

Discipleship: the best writings from the most experienced disciple makers.

    Bibliography: p.
    Contents: The vision for multiplication by Billie Hanks, Jr.—The Master and
His plan by Robert E. Coleman—Section of disciples by Robert E. Coleman— [etc.]
      1. Christian life—1960-   —Addresses, essays, lectures. I. Hanks, Billie.
II. Shell, William A.

BV4501.2.D54   253.7   81-13081
ISBN 0-310-44461-6   AACR2

Contents

FOLLOW-UP

APPRENTICESHIP

VISION

Foreword

As an evangelist I have come to see the absolute necessity of the personal follow-up of new Christians. They not only need immediate spiritual assistance, but must also have long-term growth in Christian maturity. This book is an expression of that deep concern. William A. Shell, professor of biblical studies, an editor, and an experienced disciple maker, has graciously joined me in this effort to compile the selected writings of a number of today's leading practitioners in the vital field of discipleship training.

The six additional authors whose writings have enabled us to build this anthology are respected by pastors and laypeople around the world. They are committed men who have been involved in the process of evangelism and disciple making, and their experience and quality of life commend them to the attention of the church.

After centuries of comparative silence concerning this important subject of discipleship, we are experiencing today the world-wide publication of new texts and materials dedicated to the cause of multiplication evangelism and apprenticeship. It is clear that many godly men and women are contributing to this awakened interest in and commitment to disciple making.

This anthology necessarily has to be selective. Space does not permit the listing or inclusion of many spiritual pioneers who have been active in this field and could contribute valuable insights.

The responsibility of walking with Jesus Christ in submission and commitment to Him and to His Word and the training of new Christians in the climate of love and apprenticeship are tasks for all of us to learn together and then do by the grace of God.

BILLIE HANKS, JR.
Fort Worth, Texas

Preface

THE DIVINE MANDATE

"Therefore go and make disciples of all nations" (Matt. 28:19). If this commission of our Lord is to be carried out, the principle of evangelistic multiplication commended by Paul will have to become a reality in the church: "And the things that thou hast heard of me among many witnesses, the same commit thou to faithful men, who shall be able to teach others also" (2 Tim. 2:2, KJV).

To effectively entrust the gospel to the faithful of this generation, we must act upon the Reformation message that all believers are called to be ministers. With this spiritual objective in mind, pastors and church leaders must come to see their disciple-making roles in light of Paul's words to the Ephesians: "And [God] gave some *as* apostles, and some *as* prophets, and some *as* evangelists, and some *as* pastors and teachers, for the equipping of the saints for the work of service [ministry], to the building up of the body of Christ" (Eph. 4:11-12, NASB).

This concept of ministry holds great promise for any church or individual who will take it to heart. First, we must equip our faithful, available, and teachable church members to be Christ's ministers. They must be helped to carry out the God-given work for which they were created. Paul said, "For we are God's workmanship, created in Christ Jesus to do good works, which God prepared in advance for us to do" (Eph. 2:10).

Secondly, they must be shown how to entrust spiritual

truths to faithful men and women who will then teach others. By this simple process, spiritual multiplication will begin to take place through their lives.

Thirdly, we must instill a world-wide vision in their hearts. They need to be able to see their own individual importance in God's eternal plan for world conquest. They must purpose by faith not to be weak links in God's spiritual chain, so that the witness of the gospel may soon be heard in every nation in preparation for the second coming of Jesus Christ.

Vision and a strong sense of destiny must invade our lives as we appropriate the power for witness promised by Jesus just before His ascension (see Acts 1:8), but beyond that we must also have a workable strategy. It must be one that surpasses programs and passing fads, and one that has its roots in the Scriptures. It should be no surprise that in the early church God also provided the plan and the power with the mandate to go and make disciples.

The Lost Plan

Historically it is difficult to discover why the simple plan which worked so effectively in the early church ceased to be used in later generations. We suspect that it began to be obscured after the advent of civil religion in the fourth century under Emperor Constantine. Therefore, this anthology will deal with the principles of ministry which were employed prior to that time in the earliest and most productive era of the Christian church. It is our conviction that the principles of evangelistic multiplication and apprenticeship training are indispensable if the church is to be successful in carrying out the Great Commission.

Victory Is Assured

Once a commitment to multiplication is established and the enormous potential of apprenticeship is understood, there can be no room for pessimism. As pastors and laypeople personally experience an equipping lifestyle, they develop an almost infectious commitment to training faithful men and women.

When this occurs, the church become revitalized.

The equipping concepts and spiritual disciplines described in this anthology have been applied repeatedly in many countries. In recent years, small churches, large churches, and committed individuals have established quality ministries following the examples of Jesus, Paul, Peter, and the unnamed host of early church leaders who practiced disciple making before the days of church buildings, printing presses, or mass media. Using the simplest possible tools, but the most profound strategy, they turned their generation right-side up in the cause of Christ.

The challenge of the future is simply to apply the timeless divine strategy of the past. Nothing less than total victory should be expected in world evangelization and church growth because we have the promise from the mouth of Jesus Himself: "And this gospel of the kingdom will be preached in the whole world as a testimony to all nations, and then the end will come" (Matt. 24:14).

THE EDITORS

Acknowledgments

"Association with Jesus," "The Master and His Plan," and "Selection of Disciples," by Robert E. Coleman, taken from *The Master Plan of Evangelism*, Fleming H. Revell Company (Old Tappan, N.J.), copyright © 1963, 1964 by Robert E. Coleman. Reprinted by permission of the author.

"Developing a Meaningful Relationship" and "Follow-up—An Overview," by Gary W. Kuhne, taken from *The Dynamics of Personal Follow-up*, copyright © 1976 by The Zondervan Corporation. Reprinted by permission.

Excerpts in "Character Development" and "The Need for Multiplying Disciples," by LeRoy Eims, taken from *The Lost Art of Disciple Making*, The Zondervan Corporation, copyright © 1978 by LeRoy Eims. Reprinted by permission of the author.

Excerpts in "Discipleship as a Lifestyle," by Gene Warr, taken from *You Can Make Disciples*, copyright © 1978 by Word, Inc. (Waco, Tex.). Reprinted by permission.

"Multiplying Your Efforts," by Walter A. Henrichsen, taken from *Disciples Are Made—Not Born*, Victor Books, Wheaton, Illinois, copyright © 1974 by SP Publications, Inc. Reprinted by permission.

"The Need of the Hour," by Dawson E. Trotman, taken from *The Need of the Hour*, NavPress, Colorado Springs, Colorado, © 1957, 1975 by The Navigators. Reprinted by permission.

Quotations from Scripture are from *The Holy Bible: The New International Version* unless otherwise indicated. *The New International Version* is copyright © 1973, 1978 by the New York International Bible Society. Other versions quoted in the book are the following:

AMP   *The Amplified Bible,* copyright © 1965 by Zondervan Publishing House.

ASV   *The American Standard Version,* copyright © 1901 by Thomas Nelson & Sons.

KJV   *The King James Version,* 1611.

LB   *The Living Bible,* copyright © 1971 by Tyndale House Publishers.

MLB   *The Modern Language Bible* (The Berkeley Version in Modern English), copyright © 1945 by Gerrit Verkuyl, © 1959 by Zondervan Publishing House.

NEB   *The New English Bible,* copyright © 1961, 1970 by the Delegates of the Oxford University Press and the Syndics of the Cambridge University Press.

PHILLIPS *The New Testament in Modern English, Revised,* copyright © 1958, 1960, 1972 by J. B. Phillips.

RSV   *The Revised Standard Version,* copyright © 1946, 1951, 1971 by the Division of Christian Education of the National Council of Churches of Christ in the United States of America.

Introduction

THE PURPOSE AND PLAN OF THIS BOOK

It is always hazardous to use the expression "The best" in an anthology. The best according to whom? Since there are no objective criteria necessary to judge what is the best, the choice becomes personal and emerges out of the help and effectiveness that certain writings have been in the life and ministry of the compiler.

Billie Hanks and I spent many hours praying and planning this book. We acknowledge that many other fine writings exist in this matter of discipleship and disciple making (see the *Epilog and Reading List*), but we restricted ourselves to choosing those that would be most useful in a local church-related ministry. We are committed to the proposition that discipling can and must be done at the local church level, and we believe firmly that pastors and key laypersons can be trained to be effective, reproducing disciple makers in their congregations.

With this essential philosophy in mind, we surveyed the sparse extant literature and selected these twelve chapters to include in our anthology. We looked especially for people who were practitioners of the art, not theorists, but those who are the most experienced disciple makers. We believe we are providing material that has emerged out of the lives and ministries of these men, biblical principles that have been tested in the crucible of personal experience, and concepts that will work and be effective in your given situation.

These chapters are not easy reading. They are not "nice" Christian literature that give a warm feeling inside. They are not to be read just to pass the time away or as bedtime reading. The material is "tough stuff." It is "heavy" reading. It is fraught with implications that demand obedience to God and application in daily life. Each page breathes with the challenge to greater commitment, to more involvement in the kingdom of God. The writers step on our collective toes with the clarion call "Follow my example, as I follow the example of Christ" (1 Cor. 11:1).

The book also confronts you with some choices. One choice would be to say something like, "Ho hum, so what else is new?" and go on your merry way doing nothing. Another would be to get stirred up by what you have read, determine to do something, then do nothing; sooner or later the excitement will fade away. Still another response would be to get stirred up, commit yourself to discipleship and disciple making, plan some specific things to do, then with the help of God the Holy Spirit do them—inaugurating a discipling ministry in your church, beginning to pour your life into another, and training others to a reproducing and growing ministry that will glorify Christ. We trust it will be the last.

Above all, be a noble Berean, searching "the Scriptures daily, whether those things [are] so" (Acts 17:11, KJV). Let the Holy Spirit of God using the Word of God be the instrument of your conviction. Don't become a discipler just because LeRoy Eims or Billie Hanks or Gene Warr says so; become a disciple maker because the Word of God says so and you believe that God has called you into this ministry. Then the blessing of God will be upon you, and the fruit you bear will be His.

The book is divided into five sections, each one building on the one before it. These fit the categories of the biblical basis, methodology, follow-up, apprenticeship, and vision for disciple making. They follow a progression; thus every chapter and its place in the whole is explained briefly in the introduction to that chapter, together with an introduction to the author.

So here are the best writings from the most experienced disciple makers. May you soon join their ranks.

WILLIAM A. SHELL
Grand Rapids, Michigan

1

The Vision
for Multiplication

BILLIE HANKS, JR.

The whole process of discipleship and disciple making begins with a vision. We have to see, first of all, that discipleship is the kind of life God expects of us as Christians. We are called to be followers of Jesus Christ—disciples. But we are also mandated to "go and make disciples," which is disciple making or the multiplying of disciples. And we begin by developing a biblical vision for both.

No one is better suited to help us develop that vision than Billie Hanks, Jr., who has been a practitioner of these concepts for years and is an experienced disciple maker. Through reading Dawson Trotman's *Born to Reproduce* booklet, Hanks caught the vision for spiritual multiplication, developed it into a well-honed curriculum for the local church, and has been training pastors and lay leaders on how to have and multiply a thriving discipleship ministry in the church.

Hanks is president of International Evangelism Association, a Christian service organization based in Fort Worth, Texas, and has visited more than sixty countries in the course of his evangelistic and disciple-making ministry. He holds degrees from Baylor University and Southwestern Baptist Theological Seminary and is the originator of the Christian Discipleship Seminars. He also has a summer ministry at West Texas Ranch for Christ near Sweetwater, Texas, in a discipleship training program for collegiate and seminary men and women.

Along with his preaching and training ministry, Hanks composes sacred hymns and folk songs. His popular ballad "Lonely Voices" has been a religious music best seller known around the world.

This chapter is an excerpt from an unpublished booklet titled "The Burden of My Heart," and expresses the heart and soul of a man committed to the life of discipleship and a ministry of disciple making.

1

The Vision for Multiplication

BILLIE HANKS, JR.

"And this gospel of the kingdom will be preached in the whole world as a testimony to all nations, and then the end will come" (Matt. 24:14).

On a sunny Florida afternoon years ago, I heard the haunting and unforgettable words of a leading evangelical British minister who said, "Mark my words, North American Christians: Your large church buildings will be as empty as the cathedrals of Great Britain within a span of twenty-five to fifty years if you do not change your methodology."

The well-known cleric spoke with the assurance of a prophet, yet the humility of one who had been mellowed by many years of Christian service.

Our Traditional Methodology

After hearing the English pastor speak, I decided to investigate his claims. In subsequent years I spent considerable time in England and in Europe and learned to appreciate the wisdom of his words. I discovered striking similarities between declining spiritual vitality and decreasing church membership in Great Britain decades ago and what we are seeing in large segments of the church in North America today.

We must resist the temptation to rely on the baptism of our church children to exonerate us from our larger call to national and world evangelization, and we must carefully reexamine our own methods of evangelism to see whether they

23

are based on tradition or on the Bible. Our almost exclusive dependence upon evangelism by addition through preaching is reminiscent of the days when throngs of people listened to the eloquent messages of such greats as England's Charles Haddon Spurgeon.

The academic instruction of our Christian leaders at the seminary level continues to focus on theological concepts and scholarship while all but overlooking practical instruction in how to equip laypeople for their ministries. As a result, few laypeople know how to evangelize, nurture, or disciple anyone. At a time when the world birthrate is growing faster than at any other point in history, the absence of the concept of apprenticeship in equipping the laity at the local church level all but ensures a serious, long-range decline in church membership.

One day while I was working in the Billy Graham crusade in London I was invited to lunch by one of England's leading young evangelists. Over the meal we discussed evangelism in our two countries and denominations, comparing various approaches and methods from his Anglican perspective and my Southern Baptist background.

Affter graciously complimenting my denomination as one of the world's most evangelistic, he asked me a most penetrating question: "What percentage of your Baptist laity would normally win someone to Jesus Christ during any given year?"

At that point I wished he had asked about our generous giving to missions, our popular evangelistic conferences, or our successful city-wide crusades, but he had asked a question that was most embarrassing.

I had to tell him that even in our best years fewer than 5 percent of the laity and clergy *combined* lead anyone to a saving knowledge of Christ. We simply do not have enough trained workers. We have an army of unequipped people who are sympathetic with evangelism but only a few who are participating in the joy of the harvest. Many bystanders are praying for these workers. They appreciate what the workers are doing, and even help pay their wages, but they do not know how to participate in the harvest.

As I have traveled and ministered as the guest of numerous Christian groups, I have discovered that this is the unsolved problem of evangelism world-wide. Too few are doing the work of many in evangelism. Consciously or unconsciously, we have wasted our most valuable resource: the laity.

Relying upon our traditional approach, which neglects personal follow-up and fails to utilize our more mature lay-people, we are plagued with a growing attrition rate no matter how successful our short-range evangelistic efforts appear. Because of this unattended problem, large percentages of our congregations are totally inactive and many members cannot even be found. Obviously, the new converts who never grow will never win another to Christ. It needs to be understood that evangelism's most persistent enemy is poorly planned and poorly executed follow-up.

The Evangelized as Evangelizers

The real issue involved in making disciples is international in scope and is critical in terms of the future of the church. The task of educating and motivating Christian leaders to equip the laity for a lifestyle of ministry is far larger than any single denomination, organization, or program. Something of this magnitude requires the joint effort of all Christians and a return to the biblical principles used by the early church.

Since theological education is the pacesetter in evangelism and methodology, it bears a major responsibility and obligation to be balanced, practical, and scripturally sound in its approach to disciple making. The need is urgent because the methods which we have inherited from tradition are simply not working in terms of the Great Commission. We must learn from the failures of the past and open our minds to the fact that once-Christian parts of the world now desperately need to be reevangelized. The best methods of our Reformation forefathers were not enough to sustain evangelism from generation to generation.

We must take strategic steps in our churches, colleges, and seminaries to ensure that Christians of this generation receive instruction in *how* to have a quality ministry of spiritual multiplication. Dr. Herschel H. Hobbs has wisely said, "The work of evangelism is never complete until the evangelized becomes the evangelizer." Amplifying this statement, if the process of making disciples is to be complete, all new Christians should be trained to be active in evangelism themselves. This full-circle apprenticeship process requires time, love, discipline, and personal instruction. The added work of discipleship is well worth the investment, because the fruit remains and multiplies.

The church's great evangelistic task will be carried out only when we update our philosophy of ministry through a re-examination of the principles revealed in the ministry of Christ. As we will see in detail in chapter 4, the Gospels show us that Jesus *trained* His disciples by *association* before giving them the Great Commission. Being with Him was their primary means of learning how to minister. Mark tells us, "He appointed twelve—designating them apostles—that they might be with him and that he might send them out to preach" (Mark 3:14).

The disciples' evangelism grew out of a lifestyle seasoned by many hours in Jesus' presence. They were apprenticed in real-life situations. They saw evangelism, counseling, preaching, teaching, and every other form of ministry firsthand.

Jesus' pattern was "Come, follow me, . . . and I will make you fishers of men" (Matt. 4:19). He showed them *how* to minister. By contrast, as church leaders we typically tell people *why* they ought to minister, but fail to show them *how*.

Great preaching and teaching are absolutely vital, but they cannot replace the apprenticing concept demonstrated by Christ. The critical need of the modern church does not involve moving away from preaching and teaching, but it does require reestablishing a New Testament concept of apprenticeship.

Under pastoral leadership committed to this revitalized approach, church members will be trained and shown how to carry out their God-given ministries (see Eph. 2:10). Until this happens, widespread evangelistic multiplication will not occur in the church and the average believer will never know the joy of leading another person to Christ.

Taking God's Mandate Seriously

Billy Graham has said, "One of the first verses of Scripture that Dawson Trotman, founder of the Navigators, made me memorize was 'The things that thou hast heard of me among many witnesses, the same commit thou to faithful men, who shall be able to teach others also' (2 Timothy 2:2, KJV). This is a little like a mathematical formula for spreading the gospel and enlarging the church. Paul taught Timothy; Timothy shared what he knew with faithful men; these faithful men would then teach others also. And so the process goes on and on. If every believer followed this pattern, the church could reach the entire world with the gospel in one generation! Mass crusades, in which I believe and to which I have committed my life, will never finish the Great Commission; but a one-by-one ministry will" (*The Holy Spirit*, Word Books, 1978, p. 147).

As a mass evangelist myself, I am in deep agreement with Dr. Graham that evangelism by addition alone will not reach the world. The burden of my heart is to see the concept of multiplying disciples restored to our churches again, because it alone has the realistic potential of actually reaching every nation in the world with the gospel.

Our present short-range course of action more often than not breeds a sense of frustration and spiritual fatigue in the lives of faithful Christian workers. Because of the lack of a long-range strategy, many pastors and staff members find themselves totally absorbed in a multitude of good activities to the exclusion of the best! We find no time for training our lay leaders for the work of the ministry. This omission leaves the pastor and his staff members without a strong base of qualified laypeople to labor together with them in the ministries of the local church. As a result, the paid staff carry out the church's follow-up, counseling, hospital visitation, and evangelistic ministries largely on their own.

Since many Christian workers feel that their time is too valuable for personal involvement in equipping our lay leadership, the vicious cycle repeats itself again and again. We are always too busy to follow Jesus' example. We need to come to grips with the fact that the Lord *revealed His personal pattern of ministry by investing His maximum time in the lives of those who would bear the maximum responsibility in the future ministry of the church.*

One morning I received a long distance call from a friend who pastored the largest church in his county. After three years of ministry there, he was discouraged and wanted to move on to another church field. He asked me to pray with him about the matter and to recommend him to another church if I felt led to do so.

I asked whether he had ever tried investing a portion of his time in the lives of some of his key laymen. He replied, "I don't have one layman who would be interested."

I told him I felt sure that in a congregation of five hundred there must be several persons who would respond to the challenge of one-on-one training in spiritual growth and evangelism. I then asked him why he wanted to leave.

"My people are not spiritual," he replied. "Sunday attendance fluctuates with the weather, and our Sunday school teachers are so irresponsible they do not even notify their classes when they miss."

"If that is a justification for leaving a church," I told him, "half the pastors in America would have a reason to resign." I challenged him again to start looking for a faithful man to train.

Six weeks later he called again. I will always remember his enthusiasm. He literally shouted over the phone, "Billie, praise God, I've found three men! I meet with one on Mondays, with another on Tuesdays, and with the third on Thursdays. Two are members of my church, and the third is from another church in town."

I knew the pastor of the other church and suggested that my friend obtain his permission to disciple his layman.

He laughed and said, "I've already talked with him, and he said that if I could do anything with him, I could have him!"

"Do you still want me to recommend you to another church?" I asked.

"Definitely not!" he replied. "You couldn't move me out of here with a crowbar!"

As we talked, I discovered that Sunday school had not changed, church attendance still fluctuated, and the overall circumstances were pretty much the same as before. What had changed? Three men were meeting God for a daily quiet time, memorizing Scripture, forming new priorities in their lives, and beginning to share their faith naturally as a lifestyle.

My friend was exuberant because he was now fulfilled through what was happening in these men's lives. They were the beginning of a bright new era in his ministry. Through this experience he learned to make a higher-quality investment of his time.

Our lack of training through apprenticeship leaves vast numbers of laypeople unfulfilled, because their spiritual gifts are never developed and remain unused. These people fail to receive a workable strategy for personal evangelism, so they settle into a life of churchmanship rather than disciple making. In many instances they are left wide open to an assortment of false doctrines that thrive on the biblical ignorance of immature but well-meaning church members who never received the sound instruction or loving care of a more mature Christian.

If we will learn to be *with people*, equipping them as Jesus did, and long to see new Christians perfected in Christ as Paul and Barnabas did (Acts 14:21-23), our generation can expect to see the greatest multiplication of converts and congregations since the early days of the Christian church.

Love, vision, personal discipline, and the willingness to accept mutual accountability are the critical factors needed for a lifestyle that produces spiritual multipliers. Until pastors, missionaries, and other Christian leaders take seriously God's mandate to equip His people, Christ's second coming will be postponed. His return is dependent on world evangelization (Matt. 24:14), and world evangelization is dependent on His saints being equipped for their ministries.

Every pastor and layperson can have a vital part in changing the statistics which show that we are currently losing the world. It is we who are shaping the very foundation of the future church, just as the Reformers once molded and shaped the church we love today. The awesome reality is that God has committed the spiritual destiny of the entire world to our hands. We dare not fail!

The gauntlet of leadership has been passed to our generation, and we must make an important decision regarding methodology. Every year that passes makes the right decision even more critical. A rising percentage of the world's population does not yet know Jesus Christ!

We stand at a crossroad. However good our method of addition has been, it has not been good enough. By itself, it has proved inadequate. Today's situation calls for new daring, new vision, and a return to a full-orbed New Testament philosophy of ministry. We must harness the power of evangelistic multiplication and commit ourselves to the long-range strategy of equipping all the Lord's people to be spiritual reproducers.

We have the Word of God, the Holy Spirit, two thousand years of church history, and the privilege of prayer as our resources for making the right decision.

At this moment the choice is yours! May the next two chapters by Robert Coleman be used by God to challenge you to follow Christ's example in your style of ministry.

2

The Master and His Plan

ROBERT E. COLEMAN

The question that immediately arises is whether these concepts of discipleship and disciple making are biblical, or whether they are man-devised programs of some twentieth-century groups. Robert E. Coleman gives us the biblical basis for these teachings in his masterful classic *The Master Plan of Evangelism* (Revell, 1963), a book that should hold an important place in every Christian's library.

Coleman is the McCreless Professor of Evangelism at Asbury Theological Seminary, Wilmore, Kentucky, and past president of the Academy for Evangelism in Theological Education. He is a member of the Lausanne Committee for World Evangelization and the chairman of the North American section. He is the author of many other books on Bible study and discipleship, which are read around the world in more than sixty languages. He is a graduate of Southwestern University in Texas, Asbury Theological Seminary, Princeton Theological Seminary, and the State University of Iowa, from which he received a Ph.D. degree.

Of greater import than his academic and literary accomplishments is the fact that he has been a practitioner of discipleship and disciple making. Not only has he taught in the classroom, but he has discipled many students across the years who in turn have gone on and reproduced the ministry. He has indeed practiced what he has taught and written.

Chapter 2 is excerpted from the preface to *The Master Plan of Evangelism* and calls on the reader to hark back to the first century and follow the plan of Jesus Himself in His training methodology with the twelve apostles. The Master had a master plan that worked. Read about it in Scripture with the guidance of Robert Coleman's words, then commit yourself to practicing it.

2

The Master and His Plan

ROBERT E. COLEMAN

"I am the way" *(John 14:6).*

The Problem in Evangelistic Methods

Objective and relevance—these are the crucial issues of our work. Both are interrelated, and the measure by which they are made compatible will largely determine the significance of all our activity. Merely because we are busy, or even skilled, doing something does not necessarily mean that we are getting anything accomplished. The question must always be asked: Is it worth doing? And does it get the job done?

This is a question that should be posed continually in relation to the evangelistic activity of the church. Are our efforts to keep things going fulfilling the great commission of Christ? Do we see an ever-expanding company of dedicated men reaching the world with the gospel as a result of our ministry? That we are busy in the church trying to work one program of evangelism after another cannot be denied. But are we accomplishing our objective?

Form Follows Function

Concern at this point immediately focuses on the need for a well-thought-through strategy of movement day by day in terms of the long range goal. We must know how a course of action fits into the over-all plan God has for our lives if it is to thrill our souls with a sense of destiny. This is true of any particular procedure or technique employed to propagate the gospel. Just as a building is constructed according to the plan for its use, so everything we do must have a purpose. Otherwise our activity can be lost in aimlessness and confusion.

A Study in Principles

That is why this study has been attempted. It is an effort to see controlling principles governing the movements of the Master in the hope that our own labors might be conformed to a similar pattern. As such, the book does not seek to interpret specific methods of Jesus in personal or mass evangelism. Rather this is a study in principles underlying His ministry— principles which determined His methods. One might call it a study in His strategy of evangelism around which His life was orientated while He walked on the earth.

More Research Needed

There has been surprisingly little published along this line, though, of course, most books dealing with evangelistic methods will have something to say about it in passing. The same could be said for studies in Jesus' teaching methods, as well as the general histories treating the life and work of Christ.

Probably the most careful study to date in the Master's larger plan of evangelism has been done in reference to the training of the disciples, of which A. B. Bruce's *The Training of the Twelve* is the best. First published in 1871 and revised in 1899, this narrative of the disciples' growth in the presence of the Master is still unsurpassed for wealth of insights into this subject. Another volume, *Pastor Pastorum* by Henry Latham, written in 1890, gives particular attention to Jesus' way of training men, though less comprehensive in its analysis. Since the time of these earlier studies a number of other smaller volumes have appeared which offer helpful stimulus in pursuing this theme. Not all of these works have the same evangelical theological viewpoint, but it is interesting to note that they come out at about the same place when it comes to evaluating the central thrust of Jesus' work with the disciples.

This is likewise true of numerous practical works on various phases of the church's life and ministry which have been published in recent years, most notably in the literature pertaining to the growing small group and lay witness movement in the church. While aware that these authors have not written primarily from the standpoint of evangelistic strategy, we must acknowledge our indebtedness to them for their reckoning of fundamental principles in the ministry and mission of our Lord.

However, the subject of Jesus' basic strategy has rarely been given the attention it deserves. Though we are appreciative of the labors of those who have considered it, and are not unmindful of their findings, the need for further investigation and clarification is always with us, and this is especially true of study within the primary sources themselves.

Our Plan of Study

One has to go to the New Testament, and the Gospels in particular, to really see the plan of Jesus. They are after all the only eyewitness accounts that we have of the Master at work (Luke 1:2-3; John 20:30; 21:24; 1 John 1:1). To be sure, the Gospels were written primarily to show us Christ, the Son of God, and that by faith we can have life in His name (John 20:31) But what sometimes we fail to realize is that the revelation of that life in Christ includes the way He lived and taught others so to live. We must remember that the witnesses who wrote the books not only saw the truth; they were changed by it. For this reason, in telling the story they invariably bring out those things which influenced them and others to leave all that they had to follow the Master. Not everything is reported, or course. Like any historical narrator, the gospel writers paint a picture of the whole by elaborating upon a few characteristic persons and experiences, while bringing out certain critical points in the development of events. But of those things which are carefully selected and recorded in absolute integrity under the inspiration of the Holy Spirit, we can be sure that they are intended to teach us how to follow in the way of the Master. That is why the scriptural accounts of Jesus constitute our best, and only inerrant, Textbook on Evangelism.

Hence the plan of this study has been to trace the steps of Christ as portrayed in the Gospels without undue recourse to secondary materials. In this pursuit, the inspired account of His life and work has been perused many times and from many angles trying to discern a motivating reason for the way He went about His mission. His tactics have been analyzed from the standpoint of His ministry as a whole, hoping thereby to see the larger meaning of His methods with men. Admittedly the task has not been easy, and I would be the first to acknowledge that there is more to learn. The boundless dimensions of the Lord of Glory simply cannot be confined within any human interpretation of His perfection, and the longer one looks at Him, the more he sees this to be the case.

Christ a Perfect Example

Yet recognizing this fact, there is no study more rewarding. Limited as our faculties of perception may be, we know that in the Master we have a perfect Teacher. He never made a mistake. Though partaking of our life, and being tempted in all points as we are, He was not bound by the limitations of the flesh which He accepted for our sake. Even when He did not choose to exercise His divine omniscience, His mind was clear. He always knew what was right, and as the perfect Man, He lived as God would live among men.

His Objective Was Clear

The days of His flesh were but the unfolding in time of the plan of God from the beginning. It was always before His mind. He intended to save out of the world a people for Himself and to build a church of the Spirit which would never perish. He had His sights on the day His Kingdom would come in glory and in power. This world was His by creation, but He did not seek to make it His permanent abiding place. His mansions were in the sky. He was going to prepare a place for His people that had foundations eternal in the heavens.

No one was excluded from His gracious purpose. His love was universal. Make no mistake about it. He was "the Saviour of the world" (John 4:42, ASV). God wanted all men to be saved and to come to a knowledge of the truth. To that end Jesus gave Himself to provide a salvation from all sin for all men. In that He died for one, He died for all. Contrary to our superficial thinking, there never was a distinction in His mind between home and foreign missions. To Jesus it was all world evangelism.

He Planned to Win

His life was ordered by His objective. Everything He did and said was a part of the whole pattern. It had significance because it contributed to the ultimate purpose of His life in redeeming the world for God. This was the motivating vision governing His behavior. His steps were ordered by it. Mark it well. Not for one moment did Jesus lose sight of His goal.

That is why it is so important to observe the way Jesus maneuvered to achieve His objective. The Master disclosed God's strategy of world conquest. He had confidence in the future precisely because He lived according to that plan in the present. There was nothing haphazard about His life—no wasted energy, not an idle word. He was on business for God (Luke 2:49). He lived, He died, and He rose again according to schedule. Like a general plotting His course of battle, the Son of God calculated to win. He could not afford to take a chance. Weighing every alternative and variable factor in human experience, He conceived a plan that would not fail.

Worth Careful Consideration

It is tremendously revealing to study it. Serious reflection at this point will bring the student of Christ to some profound and perhaps shattering conclusions, though the realization will likely be slow and arduous. In fact, at first glance it might even appear that Jesus had no plan. Another approach might discover some particular technique but miss the underlying pattern of it all. This is one of the marvels of His strategy. It is so unassuming and silent that it is unnoticed by the hurried churchman. But when the realization of His controlling method finally dawns on the open mind of the disciple he will be amazed at its simplicity and wonder how he could have ever failed to see it before. Nevertheless, when His plan is reflected upon, the basic philosophy is so different from that of the modern church that its implications are nothing less than revolutionary.

The following pages attempt to clarify eight guiding principles of the Master's plan. However, it must be said that the steps are not to be understood as invariably coming in this sequence, as if the last were not initiated until the others had been mastered. Actually all of the steps were implied in each one, and in some degree they all began with the first. The outline is intended only to give structure to His method and to bring out the progressive logic of the plan. One will observe that as the ministry of Jesus develops, the steps become more pronounced and the sequence more discernible.

3

Selection of Disciples

ROBERT E. COLEMAN

Where do we begin? How do we with our busy schedules, or an already overburdened pastor with his many programs, find time to disciple men and women in the local church? So many other good and important ministries cry out for our time, effort, and priorities. But let us take a few minutes to look at Jesus. He was involved in a full-time ministry, and no one can claim to be busier than He was.

Jesus spent much time and energy in preaching, teaching, healing, and performing miracles, but He spent His maximum-quality time training, apprenticing, and discipling twelve men. As Robert Coleman says, men were His method, and He concentrated on a few. What was the key to Jesus' ministry of discipling? It was the process of selection, an example that we can follow today.

This chapter is another excerpt from *The Master Plan of Evangelism* and provides a pattern we can follow practically and realistically today in our local churches and our ministry.

3

Selection
of Disciples

ROBERT E. COLEMAN

"He chose from them twelve" (Luke 6:13).

Men Were His Method

It all started by Jesus calling a few men to follow Him. This revealed immediately the direction His evangelistic strategy would take. His concern was not with programs to reach the multitudes, but with men whom the multitudes would follow. Remarkable as it may seem, Jesus started to gather these men before He ever organized an evangelistic campaign or even preached a sermon in public. Men were to be His method of winning the world to God.

The initial objective of Jesus' plan was to enlist men who could bear witness to His life and carry on His work after He returned to the Father. John and Andrew were the first to be invited as Jesus left the scene of the great revival of the Baptist at Bethany beyond the Jordan (John 1:35-40). Andrew in turn brought his brother Peter (John 1:41-42). The next day Jesus found Philip on His way to Galilee, and Philip found Nathaniel (John 1:43-51). There is no evidence of haste in the selection of these disciples; just determination. James, the brother of John, is not mentioned as one of the group until the four fishermen are recalled several months later by the Sea of Galilee (Mark 1:19; Matt. 4:21). Shortly afterward, Matthew is bidden to follow the Master as Jesus passed through Capernaum (Mark 2:13-14; Matt. 9:9; Luke 5:27-28). The particulars surrounding the call of the other disciples are not recorded in the Gospels, but it is believed that they all occurred in the first year of the Lord's ministry.

One qualification of an apostle mentioned in Acts 1:21-22 was that he should have been with Jesus, "beginning from the baptism of John, unto the day that he was received up" (ASV). Although this does not tell us from what point in John's baptismal work we are to reckon (certainly not at the beginning or from the Lord's own baptism), it does argue for an early association of all the apostles with Jesus, perhaps dating from the time of John the Baptist's imprisonment.

As one might expect, these early efforts at soul winning had little or no immediate effect upon the religious life of His day, but that did not matter greatly. For as it turned out these few early converts of the Lord were destined to become the leaders of His church that was to go with the gospel to the whole world, and from the standpoint of His ultimate purpose, the significance of their lives would be felt throughout eternity. That's the only thing that counts.

Men Willing to Learn

What is more revealing about these men is that at first they do not impress us as being key men. None of them occupied prominent places in the synagogue, nor did any of them belong to the Levitical priesthood. For the most part they were common laboring men, probably having no professional training beyond the rudiments of knowledge necessary for their vocation. Perhaps a few of them came from families of some considerable means, such as the sons of Zebedee, but none of them could have been considered wealthy. They had no academic degrees in the arts and philosophies of their day. Like their Master, their formal education likely consisted only of the synagogue schools. Most of them were raised in the poor section of the country around Galilee. Apparently the only one of the twelve who came from the more refined region of Judea was Judas Iscariot. By any standard of sophisticated culture then and now they would surely be considered as a rather ragged aggregation of souls. One might wonder how Jesus could ever use them. They were impulsive, temperamental, easily offended, and had all the prejudices of their environment. In short, these men selected by the Lord to be His assistants represented an average cross section of the lot of society in their day. Not the kind of group one would expect to win the world for Christ.

Yet Jesus saw in these simple men the potential of leadership for the kingdom. They were indeed "unlearned and ignorant" according to the world's standard (Acts 4:13), but they were teachable. Though often mistaken in their judgments and slow to comprehend spiritual things, they were honest men, willing to confess their need. Their mannerisms may have been awkward and their abilities limited, but with the exception of the traitor, their hearts were big. What is perhaps most significant about them was their sincere yearning for God and the realities of His life. The superficiality of the religious life about them had not obsessed their hope for the Messiah (John 1:41, 45, 49; 6:69). They were fed up with the hypocrisy of the ruling aristocracy. Some of them had already joined the revival movement of John the Baptist (John 1:35). These men were looking for someone to lead them in the way of salvation. Such men, pliable in the hands of the Master, could be molded into a new image—Jesus can use anyone who wants to be used.

Concentrated Upon a Few

In noting this fact, however, one does not want to miss the practical truth of how Jesus did it. Here is the wisdom of His method, and in observing it, we return again to the fundamental principle of concentration upon those He intended to use. One cannot transform a world except as individuals in the world are transformed, and individuals cannot be changed except as they are molded in the hands of the Master. The necessity is apparent not only to select a few laymen, but to keep the group small enough to be able to work effectively with them.

Hence, as the company of followers around Jesus increased, it became necessary by the middle of His second year of ministry to narrow the select company to a more manageable number. Accordingly Jesus "called His disciples, and He chose from them twelve, whom also He named apostles" (Luke 6:13-17, ASV; cf. Mark 3:13-19). Regardless of the symbolical meaning one prefers to put upon the number twelve, it is clear that Jesus intended these men to have unique privileges and responsibilities in the kingdom work.

This does not mean that Jesus' decision to have twelve apostles excluded others from following Him, for as we know, many more were numbered among His associates, and some of these became very effective workers in the church. The seventy (Luke 10:1); Mark and Luke, the gospel revelators; and James, His own brother (1 Cor. 15:7; Gal. 2:9, 12; cf. John 2:12 and 7:2-10) are notable examples of this. Nevertheless, we must acknowledge that there was a rapidly diminishing priority given to those outside the twelve.

The same rule could be applied in reverse, for within the select apostolic group Peter, James, and John seemed to enjoy a more special relationship to the Master than did the other nine. Only these privileged few are invited into the sick room of Jairus's daughter (Mark 5:37; Luke 8:51); they alone go up with the Master and behold His glory on the Mount of Transfiguration (Mark 9:2; Matt. 17:1; Luke 9:28); and amid the olive trees of Gethsemane casting their ominous shadows in the light of the full Passover moon, these members of the inner circle waited nearest to their Lord while He prayed (Mark 14:33; Matt. 26:37). So noticeable is the preference given to these three that had it not been for the incarnation of selflessness in the Person of Christ, it could well have precipitated feelings of resentment on the part of the other apostles. The fact that there is no record of the disciples complaining about the pre-eminence of the three, though they did murmur about other things, is proof that where preference is shown in the right spirit and for the right reason offense need not arise.

The Principle Observed

All of this certainly impresses one with the deliberate way that Jesus proportioned His life to those He wanted to train. It also graphically illustrates a fundamental principle of teaching: that other things being equal, the more concentrated the size of the group being taught, the greater the opportunity for effective instruction.

The principle of concentration exemplified in the ministry of Jesus was not new with Him. It had always been God's strategy from the beginning. The Old Testament records how God selected a comparatively small nation of Israel through which to effect His redemptive purpose for mankind. Even within the nation, the leadership was concentrated usually within family lines, especially the Davidic branch of the tribe of Judah.

Jesus devoted most of His remaining life on earth to these few disciples. He literally staked His whole ministry upon them. The world could be indifferent toward Him and still not defeat His strategy. It even caused Him no great concern when His followers on the fringes of things gave up their allegiance when confronted with the true meaning of the kingdom (John 6:66). But He could not bear to have His close disciples miss His purpose. They had to understand the truth and be sanctified by it (John 17:17), else all would be lost. Thus He prayed "not for the world," but for the few God gave Him "out of the world" (John 17:9, 6).

The High Priestly Prayer of Christ in the seventeenth chapter of John is especially meaningful in this connection. Of the 26 verses in the prayer, 14 relate immediately to the twelve disciples (John 17:6-19). Everything depended upon their faithfulness if the world would believe on Him "through their word" (John 17:20, ASV).

Not Neglecting the Masses

It would be wrong, however, to assume on the basis of what has here been emphasized that Jesus neglected the masses.

Such was not the case. Jesus did all that any man could be asked to do and more to reach the multitudes. The first thing He did when He started His ministry was to identify Himself boldly with the great mass revival movement of His day through baptism at the hands of John (Mark 1:9-11; Matt. 3:13-17; Luke 3:21-22), and He later went out of His way to praise this work of the great prophet (Matt. 11:7-15; Luke 7:24-28). He Himself continuously preached to the crowds that followed His miracle-working ministry. He taught them. He fed them when they were hungry. He healed their sick and cast out demons among them. He blessed their children. Sometimes the whole day would be spent ministering to their needs, even to the extent that he had "no leisure so much as to eat" (Mark 6:31, ASV). In every way possible Jesus manifested to the masses of humanity a genuine concern. These were the people that He came to save—He loved them, wept over them, and finally died to save them from their sin. No one could think that Jesus shirked mass evangelism.

Multitudes Aroused

In fact, the ability of Jesus to impress the multitudes created a serious problem in His ministry. He was so successful in expressing to them His compassion and power that they once wanted "to take Him by force, to make Him King" (John 6:15, ASV). One report by the followers of John the Baptist said that "all men" were clamoring for His attention (John 3:26). Even the Pharisees admitted among themselves that the world had gone after Him (John 12:19), and bitter as the admission must have been, the chief priests concurred in this opinion (John 11:47-48). However one looks at it, the Gospel record certainly does not indicate that Jesus lacked any popular following among the masses, despite their hesitating loyalty, and this condition lasted right on down to the end. Indeed, it was the fear of this friendly mass feeling for Jesus that prompted His accusers to capture Him in the absence of the people (Mark 12:12; Matt. 21:26; Luke 20:19).

Had Jesus given any encouragement to this popular sentiment among the masses, He easily could have had all the kingdoms of men at His feet. All He had to do was to satisfy the temporal appetites and curiosities of the people by His supernatural power. Such was the temptation presented by Satan in the wilderness when Jesus was urged to turn stones into bread and to cast Himself down from a pinnacle of the temple that God might bear Him up (Matt. 4:1-7; Luke 4:1-4, 9-13). These spectacular things would surely have excited the applause of the crowd. Satan was not offering Jesus anything when he promised Him all the kingdoms of the world if the Master would only worship him (Matt. 4:8-10). The arch deceiver of men knew full well that Jesus automatically would have this if He just turned His concentration from the things that mattered in the eternal kingdom. This is not intended to suggest that this was all that was involved in the temptation, but only to emphasize that the temptation appealed to the strategy of Jesus for world evangelism as well as to the spiritual purpose of His mission.

But Jesus would not play to the galleries. Quite the contrary. Repeatedly He took special pains to allay the superficial popular support of the multitudes which had been occasioned by His extraordinary power (e.g., John 2:23-3:3; 6:26-27). Frequently He would even ask those who were the recipients of His healing to say nothing about it in order to prevent mass demonstrations by the easily aroused multitudes. Instances of this are the case of the cleansed leper (Mark 1:44-45; Matt. 8:4; Luke 5:14-16); those freed from unclean spirits by the Sea of Galilee (Mark 3:11-12); Jairus after seeing his daughter raised from the dead (Mark 5:42-43; Luke 8:55-56); the two blind men restored to sight (Matt. 9:30); and with the blind man in Bethsaida (Mark 8:25-26).

Likewise, with the disciples following His transfiguration on the Mount "He charged them that they should tell no man what things they had seen" until after His resurrection (Mark 9:9; Matt. 17:9). On other occasions when applauded by the crowd, Jesus would slip away with His disciples and go elsewhere to continue His ministry (see John 1:29-43;

6:14-15; Mark 4:35-36; 6:1, 45-46; 7:24-8:30; Matt. 8:18, 23; 14:22-23; 15:21, 39; 16:4; Luke 5:16; 8:22).

His practice in this respect sometimes rather annoyed His followers who did not understand His strategy. Even his own brothers and sisters, who yet did not believe on Him, urged Him to abandon this policy and make an open show of Himself to the world, but He refused to take their advice (John 7:2-9).

Few Seemed to Understand

In view of this policy, it is not surprising to note that few people were actually converted during the ministry of Christ, that is, in any clear-cut way. Of course, many of the multitudes believed in Christ in the sense that His divine ministry was acceptable, but comparatively few seemed to have grasped the meaning of the gospel (see John 2:23-25; 6:30-60; 7:31-44; 11:45-46; 12:11, 17-19; Luke 14:25-35; 19:36-38; Matt. 21:8-11, 14-17; Mark 11:8-11). Perhaps His total number of devoted followers at the end of His earthly ministry numbered little more than the 500 brethren to whom Jesus appeared after the resurrection (1 Cor. 15:6), and only about 120 tarried in Jerusalem to receive the baptism of the Holy Spirit (Acts 1:15). Though this number is not small considering that His active ministry extended only over a period of three years, yet if at this point one were to measure the effectiveness of His evangelism by the number of His converts, Jesus doubtless would not be considered among the most productive mass evangelists of the church.

His Strategy

Why? Why did Jesus deliberately concentrate His life upon comparatively so few people? Had He not come to save the world? With the glowing announcement of John the Baptist ringing in the ears of multitudes, the Master easily could have had an immediate following of thousands if He wanted them. Why did He not then capitalize upon His opportunities to enlist a mighty army of believers to take the world by storm?

Surely the Son of God could have adopted a more enticing program of mass recruitment. Is it not rather disappointing that one with all the powers of the universe at His command would live and die to save the world, yet in the end have only a few ragged disciples to show for His labors?

The answer to this question focuses at once the real purpose of His plan for evangelism. Jesus was not trying to impress the crowd, but to usher in a kingdom. This meant that He needed men who could lead the multitudes. What good would it have been for His ultimate objective to arouse the masses to follow Him if these people had no subsequent supervision nor instruction in the Way? It had been demonstrated on numerous occasions that the crowd was an easy prey to false gods when left without proper care. The masses were like helpless sheep wandering aimlessly without a shepherd (Mark 6:34; Matt. 9:36; 14:14). They were willing to follow almost anyone that came along with some promise for their welfare, be it friend or foe. That was the tragedy of the hour—the noble aspirations of the people were easily excited by Jesus, but just as quickly thwarted by the deceitful religious authorities who controlled them. The spiritually blind leaders of Israel (John 8:44; 9:39-41; 12:40; cf. Matt. 23:1-39), though comparatively few in number, completely dominated the affairs of the people.

The Pharisees and Sadducees were the principal leaders of Israel, outside of the ruling Roman forces, and the whole religious, social, educational, and to a limited degree, political life of the approximately 2,000,000 people in Palestine was molded by their action. Yet the number of persons belonging to the Pharisaic guild, composed mostly of rabbis and well-to-do lay folk, according to the estimate of Josephus, did not exceed 6,000; while the total number of Sadducees, made up mostly of the chief priests and Sanhedrin families in Jerusalem, probably did not amount to more than a few hundred. When it is considered that this small privileged group of less than 7,000 people, representing about one-third of 1 percent of the population of Israel, guided the spiritual destiny of a nation, it is not difficult to see why Jesus spoke so much about them, while also teaching His disciples the strategic need for better leadership.

For this reason, unless Jesus' converts were given competent men of God to lead them on and protect them in the truth they would soon fall into confusion and despair, and the last state would be worse than the first. Thus, before the world could ever be permanently helped men would have to be raised up who could lead the multitudes in the things of God.

Jesus was a realist. He fully realized the fickleness of depraved human nature as well as the satanic forces of this world amassed against humanity, and in this knowledge He based His evangelism on a plan that would meet the need. The multitudes of discordant and bewildered souls were potentially ready to follow Him, but Jesus individually could not possibly give them the personal care they needed. His only hope was to get men imbued with His life who would do it for Him. Hence, He concentrated Himself upon those who were to be the beginning of this leadership. Though He did what He could to help the multitudes, He had to devote Himself primarily to a few men, rather than the masses, in order that the masses could at last be saved. This was the genius of His strategy.

The Principle Applied Today

Yet, strangely enough, it is scarcely comprehended in practice today. Most of the evangelistic efforts of the church begin with the multitudes under the assumption that the church is qualified to conserve what good is done. The result is our spectacular emphasis upon numbers of converts, candidates for baptism, and more members for the church, with little or no genuine concern manifested toward the establishment of these souls in the love and power of God, let alone the preservation and continuation of the work.

Surely if the pattern of Jesus at this point means anything at all it teaches that the first duty of a pastor as well as the first concern of an evangelist is to see to it that a foundation is laid in the beginning upon which can be built an effective and continuing evangelistic ministry to the multitudes. This will require more concentration of time and talents upon fewer men in the church while not neglecting the passion for the world. It will mean raising up trained leadership "for the work of ministering" with the pastor (Eph. 4:12).

This idea is brought out clearly in the translation of Ephesians 4:11 and 12 in the New English Bible, which reads: "And these were His gifts: some to be apostles, some prophets, some evangelists, some pastors and teachers, to equip God's people for work in His service, to the building up of the body of Christ." Other modern versions bring out the same essential meaning, including the Weymouth, Phillips, Wuest, Berkeley, Williams, and the Amplified New Testament. The three clauses in verse 12 are made successively dependent upon the other, with the last being the climax. According to this interpretation, Christ gave a special gift to some officials in the Church for the purpose of perfecting the saints to do the service they have each to perform in the one great goal of building up Christ's body. The ministry of the Church is seen as a work involving all members of the body (compare 1 Cor. 12:18 and 2 Cor. 9:8). A few people so dedicated in time will shake the world for God. Victory is never won by the multitudes.

Some might object to this principle when practiced by the Christian worker on the ground that favoritism is shown toward a select group in the church. But be that as it may, it is still the way that Jesus concentrated His life, and it is necessary if any permanent leadership is to be trained. Where it is practiced out of a genuine love for the whole church, and due concern is manifested toward the needs of the people, objections can at least be reconciled to the mission being accomplished. However, the ultimate goal must be clear to the worker, and there can be no hint of selfish partiality displayed in his relationships to all. Everything that is done with the few is for the salvation of the multitudes.

A Modern Demonstration

This principle of selectivity and concentration is engraved in the universe, and will bring results no matter who practices it, whether the church believes it or not. It is surely not without significance that the Communists, always alert to what works, adopted in a large measure this method of the Lord as their own. Using it to their own devious end they have multiplied from a handful of zealots seventy-five years ago to a vast conspiracy of followers that enslave nearly half the peoples of the world. They have proved in our day what Jesus demonstrated so clearly in His day that the multitudes can be won easily if they are just given leaders to follow. Is not the spread of this vicious communistic philosophy, in some measure, a judgment upon the church, not only upon our flabby commitment to evangelism, but also upon the superficial way that we have tried to go about it?

Time for Action

It is time that the church realistically faces the situation. Our days of trifling are running out. The evangelistic program of the church has bogged down on nearly every front. What is worse, the great missionary thrust of the gospel into new frontiers has largely lost its power. In most lands the enfeebled church is not even keeping up with the exploding population. All the while the satanic forces of this world are becoming more relentless and brazen in their attack. It is ironic when one stops to think about it. In an age when facilities for rapid communication of the gospel are available to the church as never before, we are actually accomplishing less in winning the world for God than before the invention of the horseless carriage.

Yet in appraising the tragic condition of affairs today, we must not become frantic in trying to reverse the trend overnight. Perhaps that has been our problem. In our concern to stem the tide, we have launched one crash program after another to reach the multitudes with the saving Word of God. But what we have failed to comprehend in our frustration is that the real problem is not with the masses—what they believe, how they are governed, whether they are fed a wholesome diet or not. All these things considered so vital are ultimately manipulated by others, and for this reason, before we can resolve the exploitation of the people we must get to those whom the people follow.

This, of course, puts a priority on winning and training those already in responsible positions of leadership. But if we can't begin at the top, then let us begin where we are and train a few of the lowly to become the great. And let us remember, too, that one does not have to have the prestige of the world in order to be greatly used in the kingdom of God. Anyone who is willing to follow Christ can become a mighty influence upon the world providing, of course, this person has the proper training himself.

Here is where we must begin just like Jesus. It will be slow, tedious, painful, and probably unnoticed by men at first, but the end result will be glorious, even if we don't live to see it. Seen this way, though, it becomes a big decision in the ministry. One must decide where he wants his ministry to count—in the momentary applause of popular recognition or in the reproduction of his life in a few chosen men who will carry on his work after he has gone. Really it is a question of which generation we are living for.

But we must go on. It is necessary now to see how Jesus trained His men to carry on His work. The whole pattern is part of the same method, and we cannot separate one phase from the other without destroying its effectiveness.

4

Association
With Jesus

ROBERT E. COLEMAN

How do we get started? The answer to this is another question, How did Jesus do it? His methodology was to spend quality time with His disciples, pouring His life into theirs. To do this, He had to be with them, and this is the concept of association.

Robert Coleman discusses the biblical basis for the ministry of association in the second chapter of *The Master Plan of Evangelism,* presented here as our chapter 4. Jesus had a thriving public ministry, but the real work of preparing His disciples for the task that would soon be theirs was done in private. He totally associated Himself with the Twelve, making out of them the disciples and disciple makers they became after His ascension.

(The other chapters of Coleman's classic should be read as well. They deal with the topics of consecration, impartation, demonstration, delegation, supervision, and reproduction, and are essentially methodological. So obtain the book, read carefully, enjoy thoroughly, then go out and practice its concepts zealously.)

4

Association With Jesus

ROBERT E. COLEMAN

"Lo, I am with you always" (Matt. 28:20).

He Stayed With Them

Having called his men, Jesus made it a practice to be with them. This was the essence of His training program—just letting His disciples follow Him.

When one stops to think of it, this was an incredibly simple way of doing it. Jesus had no formal school, no seminaries, no outlined course of study, no periodic membership classes in which He enrolled His followers. None of these highly organized procedures considered so necessary today entered at all into His ministry. Amazing as it may seem, all Jesus did to teach these men His way was to draw them close to Himself. He was His own school and curriculum.

The natural informality of this teaching method of Jesus stood in striking contrast to the formal, almost scholastic procedures of the scribes. These religious teachers of His day insisted upon their disciples adhering strictly to certain rituals and formulas of knowledge, whereby they were distinguished from others; whereas Jesus asked only that His disciples follow Him. Knowledge was not communicated by the Master in terms of laws and dogmas, but in the living personality of One who walked among them. His disciples were distinguished, not by outward conformity to certain rituals, but by being with Him, and thereby participating in His doctrine (John 18:19).

57

now Was to Be With

It was by virtue of this fellowship that the disciples were permitted "to know the mysteries of the Kingdom of God" (Luke 8:10, ASV). Knowledge was gained by association before it was understood by explanation. This was no better expressed than when one of the band asked, "How know we the way," reflecting his frustration at the thought of the Holy Trinity. Whereupon Jesus replied: "I am the way, the truth, and the life" (John 14:5-6, ASV), which was to say that the point in question already was answered, if the disciples would but open their eyes to the spiritual reality incarnated in their midst.

This simple methodology was revealed from the beginning by the invitation that Jesus gave to those men whom He wanted to lead. John and Andrew were invited to "come and see" the place where Jesus stayed (John 1:39). Nothing more was said, according to the Record. Yet what more needed to be said. At home with Jesus they could talk things over and there in private see intimately into His nature and work. Philip was addressed in the same essential manner, "Follow me" (John 1:43). Evidently impressed by this simple approach, Philip invited Nathaniel also to "come and see" the Master (John 1:46). One living sermon is worth a hundred explanations. Later when James, John, Peter, and Andrew were found mending their nets, Jesus reminded them in the same familiar words, "Come ye after Me," only this time adding the reason for it, "and I will make you fishers of men" (Mark 1:17, ASV; cf. Matt. 4:19; Luke 5:10). Likewise, Matthew was called from the seat of custom with the same invitation, "Follow me" (Mark 2:14; Matt. 9:9; Luke 5:27).

The Principle Observed

See the tremendous strategy of it. By responding to this initial call believers in effect enrolled themselves in the Master's school where their understanding could be enlarged and their faith established. There were certainly many things which these men did not understand—things which they themselves freely acknowledged as they walked with Him; but all these problems could be dealt with as they followed Jesus. In His presence they could learn all that they needed to know.

This principle which was implied from the start was given specific articulation later when Jesus chose from the larger group about Him the twelve "that they might be with Him" (Mark 3:14, ASV; cf. Luke 6:13). He added, of course, that He was going to send them forth "to preach, and to have authority to cast out devils," but often we fail to realize what came first. Jesus made it clear that before these men were "to preach" or "to cast out devils" they were to be "with Him." In fact, this personal appointment to be in constant association with Him was as much a part of their ordination commission as the authority to evangelize. Indeed, it was for the moment even more important, for it was the necessary preparation for the other.

Closer As Training Ends
The determination with which Jesus sought to fulfill this commission is evident as one reads through the subsequent gospel accounts. Contrary to what one might expect, as the ministry of Christ lengthened into the second and third years He gave increasingly more time to the chosen disciples, not less. Some scholars have contended that, prior to ordination of the apostles, Jesus' first concern was with the multitudes while afterward the emphasis shifted to the disciples, and especially to the Twelve. Whether such a decisive division of concern is justified from the record or not, the fact is clear that Jesus did increasingly give Himself to the apostolic company as time went on.

Frequently He would take them with Him in a retreat to some mountainous area of the country where He was relatively unknown seeking to avoid publicity as far as possible. They took trips together to Tyre and Sidon to the northwest (Mark 7:24; Matt. 15:21); to the "borders of Decapolis" (Mark 7:31; cf. Matt. 15:29) and "the parts of Dalmanutha" to the southeast of Galilee (Mark 8:10; cf. Matt. 15:39); and to the "villages of Caesarea Philippi" to the northeast (Mark 8:27; cf.

Matt. 16:13). These journeys were made partly because of the opposition of the Pharisees and the hostility of Herod, but primarily because Jesus felt the need to get alone with His disciples. Later He spent several months with His disciples in Perea east of the Jordan (Luke 13:22-19:28; John 10:40-11:54; Matt. 19:1-20:34; Mark 10:1-52). As opposition mounted there, Jesus "walked no more openly among the Jews, but departed thence into the country near to the wilderness, into a city called Ephraim; and there He tarried with His disciples" (John 11:54). When at last the time came for Him to go to Jerusalem, He significantly "took the twelve disciples apart" from the rest as He made His way slowly to the city (Matt. 20:17, ASV; cf. Mark 10:32).

In view of this, it is not surprising that during passion week Jesus scarcely ever let His disciples out of His sight. Even when He prayed alone in Gethsemane, His disciples were only a stone's throw away (Luke 22:41). Is not this the way it is with every family as the hour of departing draws near? Every minute is cherished because of the growing realization that such close association in the flesh soon will be no more. Words uttered under these circumstances are always more precious. Indeed, it was not until time began to close in that the disciples of Christ were prepared to grasp many of the deeper meanings of His presence with them (John 16:4). Doubtless this explains why the writers of the Gospels were constrained to devote so much of their attention to these last days. Fully half of all that is recorded about Jesus happened in the last months of His life, and most of this in the last week.

The course followed by Jesus through life was supremely portrayed in the days following His resurrection. Interestingly enough, every one of the ten post-resurrection appearances of Christ was to His followers, particularly the chosen apostles.

This fact was impressively recognized by the disciples, as Peter said: "Him God raised up the third day, and gave Him to be made manifest, not to all the people, but unto witnesses that were chosen before of God, even to us who did eat and drink with Him after He rose from the dead" (Acts 10:40-41, ASV).

So far as the Bible shows, not a single unbelieving person was permitted to see the glorified Lord. Yet it is not so strange. There was no need to excite the multitudes with His spectacular revelation. What could they have done? But the disciples who had fled in despair following the crucifixion needed to be revived in their faith and confirmed in their mission to the world. His whole ministry evolved around them.

And so it was. The time which Jesus invested in these few disciples was so much more by comparison to that given to others that it can only be regarded as a deliberate strategy. He actually spent more time with His disciples than with everybody else in the world put together. He ate with them, slept with them, and talked with them for the most part of His entire active ministry. They walked together along the lonely roads; they visited together in the crowded cities; they sailed and fished together in the Sea of Galilee; they prayed together in the deserts and in the mountains; and they worshiped together in the synagogues and in the temple.

Still Ministering to the Masses

One must not overlook, too, that even while Jesus was ministering to others, the disciples were always there with Him. Whether He addressed the multitudes that pressed upon Him, conversed with the scribes and Pharisees who sought to ensnare Him, or spoke to some lonely beggar along the road, the disciples were close at hand to observe and to listen. In this manner, Jesus' time was paying double dividends. Without neglecting His regular ministry to those in need, He maintained a constant ministry to His disciples by having them with Him. They were thus getting the benefit of everything He said and did to others plus their own personal explanation and counsel.

It Takes Time

Such close and constant association, of course, meant virtually that Jesus had no time to call His own. Like little children clamoring for the attention of their father, the disciples were always under foot of the Master. Even the time He took to go apart to keep His personal devotions was subject to interruption at the disciples' need (Mark 6:46-48; cf. Luke 11:1). But Jesus would have it no other way. He wanted to be with them. They were His spiritual children (Mark 10:24; John 13:33; 21:5), and the only way that a father can properly raise a family is to be with them.

The Foundation of Follow-up

Nothing is more obvious yet more neglected than the application of this principle. By its very nature, it does not call attention to itself, and one is prone to overlook the commonplace. Yet Jesus would not let His disciples miss it. During the last days of His journey, the Master especially felt it necessary to crystallize in their thinking what He had been doing. For example, once turning to those who had followed Him for three years, Jesus said: "Ye (shall) bear witness because ye have been with me from the beginning" (John 15:27). Without any fanfare and unnoticed by the world, Jesus was saying that He had been training men to be His witnesses after He had gone, and His method of doing it was simply by being "with them." Indeed, as He said on another occasion, it was because they had "continued with" Him in His temptations that they were appointed to be leaders in His eternal kingdom where they would each eat and drink at His table, and sit on thrones judging the twelve tribes of Israel (Luke 22:28-30).

It would be wrong to assume, however, that this principle of personal follow-up was confined only to the apostolic band. Jesus concentrated Himself upon these few chosen men, but to a lesser and varying degree He manifested the same concern with others that followed Him. For example, He went home with Zaccheus after his conversion on the street of Jericho (Luke 19:7), and He spent some time with him before leaving the city. After the conversion of the woman at the well in Samaria, Jesus tarried two extra days in Sychar to instruct the men of that community who "believed on Him because of the word of the woman who testified," and because of that personal association with them "many more believed," not because of the woman's witness, but because they heard for themselves the Master (John 4:39-42). Often one who received some help from the Master would be permitted to join the procession following Jesus, as for example, Bartimaeus (Mark 10:52; Matt. 20:34; Luke 18:43). In such a way many attached themselves to the apostolic company, as is evidenced by the seventy with Him in the later Judean ministry (Luke 10:1, 17). All of these believers received some personal attention, but it could not be compared to that given to the Twelve.

Mention should be made, too, of that small group of faithful women who ministered to Him out of their substance, like Mary and Martha (Luke 10:38-42), Mary Magdalene, Joanna, Susanna, "and many others" (Luke 8:1-3). Some of these women were with Him to the end. He certainly did not refuse their gracious kindness and often took the occasion to help them in their faith. Nevertheless, Jesus was well aware of the sex barrier, and although He welcomed their assistance, He did not try to incorporate these ladies into the select company of His chosen disciples. There are limitations in this kind of follow-up which one must recognize.

But apart from the rules of propriety, Jesus did not have the time to personally give all these people, men or women, constant attention. He did all that He could, and this doubtless served to impress upon His disciples the need for immediate personal care of new converts, but He had to devote Himself primarily to the task of developing some men who in turn could give this kind of personal attention to others.

The Church As a Continuing Fellowship
Really the whole problem of giving personal care to every believer is only resolved in a thorough understanding of the nature and mission of the church. It is well here to observe that the emergence of the church principle around Jesus, whereby one believer was brought into fellowship with all

others, was the practice in a larger dimension of the same thing that He was doing with the Twelve.

One cannot help but observe in this connection that the references to "the disciples" as a corporate body are much more frequent in the Gospels than are references to an individual disciple. When it is remembered that these accounts were written under inspiration by the disciples, and not Jesus, it is quite significant that they would set forth their own place in such terms. We need not infer from this that the disciples were unimportant as individuals, for such was not the case, but it does impress us with the fact that the disciples understood their Lord to look upon them as a body of believers being trained together for a common mission. They saw themselves through Christ first as a church and secondly as individuals within that body.

Actually it was the church that was the means of following up all those who followed Him. That is, the group of believers became the body of Christ, and as such ministered to each other individually and collectively.

Every member of the community of faith had a part to fulfill in this ministry. But this they could only do as they themselves were trained and inspired. As long as Jesus was with them in the flesh, He was the Leader, but thereafter, it was necessary for those in the church to assume this leadership. Again this meant that Jesus had to train them to do it, which involved His own constant personal association with a few chosen men.

Our Problem

When will the church learn this lesson? Preaching to the masses, although necessary, will never suffice in the work of preparing leaders for evangelism. Nor can occasional prayer meetings and training classes for Christian workers do this job. Building men is not that easy. It requires constant personal attention, much like a father gives to his children. This is something that no organization or class can ever do. Children are not raised by proxy. The example of Jesus would teach us that it can only be done by persons staying right with those they seek to lead.

The church obviously has failed at this point, and failed tragically. There is a lot of talk in the church about evangelism and Christian nurture, but little concern for personal association when it becomes evident that such work involves the sacrifice of personal indulgence. Of course, most churches insist on bringing new members through some kind of a confirmation class which usually meets an hour a week for a month or so. But the rest of the time the young convert has no contact at all with a definite Christian training program, except in worship services and the Sunday school. Unless the new Christian, if indeed he is saved, has parents or friends who will fill the gap in a real way, he is left on his own to find the solutions to innumerable practical problems, any one of which could mean disaster to his faith.

With such haphazard follow-up of believers, it is no wonder that about half of those who make professions and join the church eventually fall away or lose the glow of a Christian experience, and fewer still grow in sufficient knowledge and grace to be of any real service to the kingdom. If Sunday services and membership training classes are all that a church has to develop young converts into mature disciples, then they are defeating their own purpose by contributing to a false security, and if the person follows the same lazy example, it may ultimately do more harm than good. There is simply no substitute for getting with people, and it is ridiculous to imagine that anything less, short of a miracle, can develop strong Christian leadership. After all, if Jesus, the Son of God, found it necessary to stay almost constantly with His few disciples for three years, and even one of them was lost, how can a church expect to do this job on an assembly line basis a few days out of the year?

The Principle Applied Today

Clearly the policy of Jesus at this point teaches us that whatever method of follow-up the church adopts, it must have as its basis a personal guardian concern for those entrusted to their care. To do otherwise is esentially to abandon new believers to the devil.

This means that some system must be found whereby every convert is given a Christian friend to follow until such time as he can lead another. The counselor should stay with the new believer as much as possible, studying the Bible and praying together, all the while answering questions, clarifying the truth, and seeking together to help others. If a church does not have such committed counselors willing to do this service, then it should be training some. And the only way they can be trained is by giving them a leader to follow.

This answers the question of how it is to be done, but it is necessary now to understand that this method can accomplish its purpose only when the followers practice what they learn. Hence, another basic principle in the Master's strategy must be understood.

5

The Need for Multiplying Disciples

LEROY EIMS

If we are convinced that God wants us in a discipling ministry because it has a firm biblical basis, then how do we go about having one? This next section of three chapters deals with some methodology from the pens of three experienced disciple makers who have practiced this ministry in three different contexts.

If we believe that the Bible teaches this concept and that we are called of God to have this ministry, then we need to be firm in our minds that we should have a *multiplying* ministry of disciple making. No one is better suited to lead us into thinking that way and practicing what we think than LeRoy Eims, assistant to the president of The Navigators. He has been practicing what he writes about for more than thirty years.

Eims is a popular and effective speaker at conferences and has ministered in churches, seminaries, and Bible schools and to students, servicemen, and adults in all parts of the world, including behind the Iron Curtain. He is the author of books on Christian leadership, Christian living, and discipleship. This chapter is excerpted from his first chapter in *The Lost Art of Disciple Making* (Zondervan, 1978).

One of Eims's gifts is being able to illustrate biblical truths and concepts with vivid, down-to-earth, contemporary illustrations. We used to call these "war stories," and Eims—with his experience in the United States Marine Corps in World War II and many years of productive ministry to servicemen with The Navigators—has a myriad of them. This chapter contains some classic stories of how disciple making really works in our time; what happened in the lives of Joe, Johnny, Roy, and LeRoy himself are unforgettable and challenging to all of us. So let us be challenged and commit ourselves to having this kind of methodology in our own ministry.

5

The Need for
Multiplying Disciples

LEROY EIMS

*"And the word of God increased; and the number of the disciples
multiplied in Jerusalem greatly"* (Acts 6:7, KJV).

One day I received a phone call from a busy pastor. Could we
get together, he asked, someplace, sometime to talk about
training people in his church? He was willing to fly anywhere
in the United States to meet me and discuss his problem for
half a day or so. He obviously needed help, so we set up a
meeting.

As we spent some time together, I found his situation to be
fairly typical. He was the pastor of a growing, healthy, and
flourishing church. People were coming to Christ, attendance
had increased, and he had to have two morning worship services. God was clearly blessing in many wonderful ways.

But he also had a problem. He knew that unless he trained
some spiritually qualified workers among the men and women
of his congregation, many people would not get needed help
in the initial stages of Christian growth (adequate follow-up)
and would not develop into strong, robust disciples of Jesus
Christ. And the pastor knew he was the key to this. The
whole process had to begin with him. He could not toss it to a
"department," nor delegate it to someone else. As the spiritual leader of these people, he had to lead the way.

He had another problem—he was already a busy man.
Many things demanded his attention; many people demanded
his time. Like many pastors, he spent a good deal of his time

putting out brush fires in his congregation. No sooner had he dealt with one problem than another one arose.

To his consternation and frustration, he spent too much time with problem-centered people, trying to settle quarrels, make peace between members, deal with difficult family situations, and a hundred and one other things.

But he had a dream. At times, he would go into his study, lock the door, and think of his situation in a whole new light. *Wouldn't it be great,* he would think to himself, *if I had a dedicated, ever-growing band of spiritually qualified men and women who could help handle some of the "spiritual" problems that keep coming up in this church?*

He did not mean people who merely took tapes of his sermons to the shut-ins, delivered food, clothing, and financial aid to the needy, taught in the Sunday school, or helped him manage the business and financial affairs of the church. He meant people who knew how to win another person to Christ and then take that person from the time of his conversion and help him become a solid, dedicated, committed, fruitful, mature disciple who could in time repeat that process in the life of another.

He would smile there in the privacy of his study, for his dream was so vivid he could almost reach out and touch that which he envisioned. But then he would be jarred back to reality by the ringing of the phone. Another problem. And he was the only spiritually qualified person in the congregation who could help. So he would set aside his dream, pick up his Bible, and go out the door.

Disciples in Action

Let's look at another scene. Four couples are meeting for a Bible study on a weeknight. They have been getting together for about four months, since three of them had been converted to Christ. One of the laymen in the church has been leading the study, and they have just settled down for one of their lively discussions. As they launch into their lesson, the phone rings.

"Is Joe there?" Joe is one of the four-month-old Christians. "Yes, but he's busy right now. He's in a Bible study." The voice is desperate. "Please! I've got to talk with him." "OK."

Joe picks up the phone and listens. "OK," he says, "I'll come right over."

Joe comes back to his Bible study group and explains. His business partner wants him to come over and help him. There's been a marital fight, and the man's wife is walking out on him. The whole mess has been brewing for a long time, and Joe feels he should go and do what he can.

The leader of the study group says he thinks it's the right thing to do, and while Joe's gone the group will pray. So Joe, a four-month-old Christian, picks up his Bible and goes out the door to try to save a marriage. The Bible study turns into a prayer meeting.

That scene is a real situation with real people. The leader of that group told me about it a few days after it happened. At the time he hadn't heard from Joe on how his meeting with his partner had gone. I saw that leader again about three weeks later and heard the great news. Joe had been used of God to lead both husband and wife to Christ. He was now in the process of leading them in a study of the Scriptures.

The leader, in turn, had begun to spend a little extra time with Joe to answer some of his questions now that he and his wife were leading new Christians in a study of the Word of God. Though Joe had always been eager, he was more so now. He needed a great deal of help and knew it. The leader was only too glad to do what he could. He could see that the Lord was using that time to deepen their relationship and to deepen Joe's life in the Lord.

It was also a challenge to the other couples in Joe's study group. It had become evident to them that sooner or later the Lord would give them an opportunity to share with others some of the things they were learning. It made the study that much more meaningful to all of them.

That scene, with variations, is being repeated in many

places around the world. It is not an isolated incident. In fact, the story of the pastor who met with me, mentioned earlier in this chapter, has a happy ending. After we'd spent the day together discussing making disciples and training workers, he went back to his church and began putting into practice the principles which I shared with him and which are taught in this book.

Today, there is a steady stream of disciples and workers who emerge from his ministry to affect their neighborhoods and friends for Christ. These people from his church are being used of God to win others to Christ and to help their converts, in turn, repeat the process.

This concept of multiplying disciples has not always been so widely accepted as it is today. At one time, in fact, not too long ago, relatively few people were doing it. But many more today are returning to that biblical process.

The Crucial Element of Personal Help

Shortly after my wife, Virginia, and I became Christians, we met Waldron Scott, a young man about our age who took a personal interest in us. He had been helped in his Christian life by a fellow serviceman while he was stationed on Guam with the Air Force in World War II. We were classmates in college, and he came over to our home once a week or so to share spiritual truths with us and to help us in our growth.

His actual working with us began on the day I asked him why there seemed to be such an obvious difference in our Christian lives, why he was like he was and Virginia and I were like we were. He was able to quote the Scriptures like he knew them by heart; fairly regularly he would share how God had answered his prayers; he seemed to know his Bible well.

He came over that night and asked me some questions. Did I read my Bible regularly? No, hardly ever. Did I study it? Again, no. Did I memorize it? Aha, here I had him. The previous Sunday our pastor had preached on Matthew 6:33, and I had been so impressed by the verse that I memorized it when I got home.

"Great," Scotty said. "Quote it for me. Let's hear it."

I couldn't remember it. I realized then that there was something lacking in my Scripture memory program.

Then he asked, "Do you pray?"

"Well, yes," I told him. "At mealtimes I repeat a prayer I have memorized." We were just sitting down for some refreshments, so I said my prayer: "Bless the food which now we take, to do us good for Jesus' sake. Amen."

During the course of the evening it became obvious that there was much more to prayer than that. He offered to meet with my wife and me and share some of the things that had been of help to him. We were eager to do so.

We began. Scotty taught us how to read the Bible and get something out of our reading. He taught us how to do personal Bible study and, with the help of the Holy Spirit, apply its lessons to our lives. He taught us to memorize the Word so that it would be available to the Holy Spirit twenty-four hours a day. He taught us how to assimilate the Scriptures into the spiritual bloodstream of our lives through meditation on the Word. He taught us how to pray and expect answers from God. That was a blessed year for us. We were eager to learn, and Scotty was willing to spend time with us.

The next year I began my sophomore year and Scotty continued to meet with us. We were continuing to grow and my Christian life was full of new discoveries. We had discovered the high adventure of abundant Christian living, as the Lord was becoming more personal and real in our lives.

Midway through the first semester, a classmate came up to me and said, "You know, LeRoy, I've been watching you. Your Christian life is sure on a different plane than mine." And he began asking some questions, essentially what I had asked Scotty the year before.

I smiled. "Well, do you read your Bible regularly?"

"No."

"Do you study it?" No again.

"Do you memorize the Scriptures?" No, he didn't do that either.

"Do you pray?" Still no.

I suggested we get together and talk about these things. He was eager and enthusiastic, so we began. I shared with him the things Scotty had shared with me, and he began to grow in his Christian life. He began to dig into the Word, pray, witness, and the Spirit of God worked mightily in his life that year.

The following year I transferred to the University of Washington, and my friend transferred to another school. A few months after school began I received an interesting letter from him. He had been attending a Christian fellowship on campus and a fellow student had come up to him and asked him about his Christian life. It seemed this student had noticed a difference and wanted to find out about it. So my friend asked him some questions that had to do with Bible reading, study, memory, and prayer. He had shown a keen interest in doing these things, so my friend had begun to share with him on a regular basis the things he had learned from me and which I had learned from Scotty.

Meanwhile, a Christian student had come up to me on the University of Washington campus . . . and so it goes. For many years now I have been involved in helping others personally in their Christian lives. I've watched the interest pastors, missionaries, dedicated laymen, college and seminary students, and servicemen have shown in helping others individually as well. Today a growing groundswell of interest in multiplying disciples is to be seen in many churches and by many people.

To Multiply or Not to Multiply—That Is the Question

Some years ago I was talking to a zealous young Christian. "Bob," I asked, "what's the thing that brings you more joy than anything else in life?"

"Man, LeRoy, that's easy," he replied. "Leading someone to Christ."

I agreed with him. Everybody is happy when that happens —you are happy, the new convert is happy, there is joy in heaven. "But there is something even greater than that."

He was puzzled. What could possibly be greater than seeing a person come to Christ?

I continued, "When the person you have led to Christ grows and develops into a dedicated, fruitful, mature disciple who then goes on to lead others to Christ and help them in turn as well."

"Say!" he exclaimed, "I've never thought of that!"

Frankly, it is no surprise that he hadn't heard or thought of that. In those days the idea was pretty obscure, but he was willing to take the time to learn, and he did. Today there are many mature, committed, fruitful disciples on two continents because of the impact of Bob's life and his vision of multiplying disciples.

On the other hand, a lack of knowledge of these things can have sad consequences. I was visiting a foreign mission field and spoke with a veteran missionary. He told me a story that still haunts me; I can't get it out of my mind. It seems that he went overseas some fifteen years before we met and began the usual programs. About the time he arrived on his field, he met a young man named Johnny, who was involved in something quite different.

Johnny was a committed disciple of Jesus Christ, but he was going about his ministry in all the wrong ways according to the "book." In contrast to the typical missionary approach of the time, Johnny was spending the bulk of his time meeting with a few young men in that country. The veteran missionary tried to get Johnny straightened out, but the young man kept on with his "different" approach. The years passed, and the veteran missionary now had to leave the country of his service due to new visa restrictions.

As he sat across the coffee table from me in his home, he told me, "LeRoy, I've got little to show for my time there. Oh, there is a group of people who meet in our assembly, but I wonder what will happen to them when I leave. They are not disciples. They have been faithful in listening to my sermons, but they do not witness. Few of them know how to lead another person to Christ. They know nothing about discipling others. And now that I am leaving, I can see I've all but wasted my time here."

He continued, "Then I look at what has come out of Johnny's life. One of the men he worked with is now a professor at the university. This man is mightily used of God to reach and train scores of university students. Another is leading a witnessing and discipling team of about forty young men and women. Another is in a nearby city with a group of thirty-five growing disciples around him. Three have gone to other countries as missionaries and are now leading teams who are multiplying disciples. God is blessing their work.

"I see the contrast between my life and his and it is tragic. I was so sure I was right. What he was doing seemed so insignificant, but now I look at the results and they are staggering." It was a sad meeting for both of us.

On another occasion I was speaking at a weekend conference in the Midwest. A pastor who had spent the bulk of his life as a missionary in the Middle East and was now in a nearby city came to the conference. In the opening meeting, I shared this passage with the conferees: "It was he who gave some to be apostles, some to be prophets, some to be evangelists, and some to be pastors and teachers, to prepare God's people for works of service, so that the body of Christ may be built up" (Eph. 4:11-12, KJV).

I tried to explain that the thrust of that passage was that God had given leaders to the church in order to build up and train the rest of us in the work of the ministry. I said that the ministry of the gospel was to be done by all of us—laymen and clergy alike. All of us together are to be a great witnessing brotherhood, but we need training.

After the meeting this man came up to me and held out his Greek New Testament. "That's exactly what it says," he stated.

With that he turned and walked away, went to his room, packed his bags, and started to leave the conference. I was startled by his actions, so I stopped him and asked if we had offended him in some way. Was there anything for which we should apologize and ask his forgiveness?

"Not at all," he replied. "I've got all I need. My people are going to hear about this!" With that he got into his car and drove off. He simply wanted to be back with his people that very Sunday, preach to them that very message, and begin practicing it in his ministry.

In recent years I have watched the country where he had served for so many years blow up with bitter hatreds and racial strife. I've often wondered if it might have been a different story had he gone there thirty years ago with the vision of discipling a band of men and women, something like Johnny had done on another mission field.

One spring a colleague of mine and I taught a workshop at a seminary in their School of Evangelism. The workshop ran for three days, was about two-and-a-half hours long, and was well attended. Our topic was "Discipleship in the Local Church."

During one of our discussion sessions, an elderly pastor spoke up and told us of his own experience in discipling some of the men in his church. He had started this about three years before and now had a band of stalwart, faithful men on whom he could call at a moment's notice. He had started with one man; later he and this man worked with two others who had expressed interest. The discipling process continued, and after a time the four of them began to meet with four others. The ministry had multiplied till he now had this dedicated band of men who were truly spiritually qualified to work in the ministry of the church.

The elderly pastor told us it was by far the most rewarding, fulfilling, and exciting thing that had happened to him in thirty-five years in the ministry. After this account, the eyes of many of the young seminarians began to gleam with anticipation. They could hardly wait to get out into the pastorate and begin their own ministry of multiplying disciples.

The Indianapolis Model

Dr. Roy Blackwood has been a close personal friend of mine for years. He has been multiplying disciples since he went to Indianapolis, Indiana, to form a new congregation in his denomination. He determined to build his ministry on this philosophy of training men to train others in discipleship and in making disciples.

He did not want to be just a Bible teacher to a group of spiritually hungry souls who would get their only ration of spiritual food once a week from his sermons. He wanted to train a band of strong, rugged soldiers of the Cross who would then collaborate with him in the work of the ministry in the church.

Some years have now passed and his ministry has proved to be one of the unique expressions of discipleship in our day. Roy has his disciples. In fact, when he and his wife went around the world on a preaching and lecture tour, he left the church in the able hands of the people whom he had trained and was gone for almost a year.

During his absence, the men preached the sermons and directed the activities of the church. They *did* the ministry and the Lord blessed their efforts as the congregation grew and flourished under their leadership. When Roy and his wife returned from their trip, he wondered if there could still be a place and a need for him. There was, of course, but he would work with the others in the ministry of multiplying disciples.

Some years ago a man came to me with what he thought was a great idea. He was bubbling over with enthusiasm and was eager to secure my participation in his plan to forward the work of Christ. So I listened carefully. When he had finished, I declined his offer to become involved. He was surprised and asked why I would not work with him.

"Two reasons," I replied. "One, it is not scriptural. Two, it won't work."

What I enjoy so much about the ministry of multiplying disciples is that it is scriptural and it works. It is a scriptural approach to helping fulfill Christ's Great Commission (Matt. 28:18-20), and helping to do something about training workers (Matt. 9:37-38) who today, as in Christ's day, are still few.

Second, I have seen it in action for over twenty-five years and it works. When some of us were involved in a ministry of multiplying disciples in the 1950s, we didn't have it well codified and organized. We just called it "working with a few men (or women)." But since those days I've watched pastors, housewives, missionaries, nurses, building contractors, school teachers, seminary professors, and grocery owners get involved in the lives of a few people. I have seen the Lord bless their efforts and multiply their lives in Christ into the lives of others.

This is not a cure-all, of course, but few things are. But I do know this. When you start spending individual time with another Christian for the purpose of having a ministry in his or her life—time together in the Word, prayer, fellowship, systematic training—something happens in your own life as well. May God grant you patience, love, and perseverance as you begin to share the life He has given you with others.

6

Multiplying Your Efforts

WALTER A. HENRICHSEN

Walter A. Henrichsen is a master teacher, and he is equally proficient in person and in his writings. He has the gift of being able to present biblical truths systematically and point by point in such a way that they are easily remembered and practically applicable in discipleship ministry. He may not tell as many "war stories" as LeRoy Eims, but his careful exposition of the biblical data will give us some practical methodology to take back with us into our ministry.

⚹ Henrichsen is a graduate of Western Theological Seminary in Holland, Michigan, and was associated with The Navigators for many years. He now works with Leadership Foundation, helping business and professional people fulfill their discipleship potential for Jesus Christ in the context of their own fields. Residing in Colorado Springs, Colorado, he travels to major business centers throughout the United States and around the world, training businessmen and professionals to have a discipling ministry that multiplies their efforts.

Chapter 6 is taken from Henrichsen's bestselling *Disciples Are Made—Not Born* (Victor, 1974), one of the first books on discipleship to appear in this time of rediscovery of this biblical concept. It is still one of the best treatments of the whole topic and worthwhile including in a personal library.

6

Multiplying Your Efforts

WALTER A. HENRICHSEN

"Be fruitful and multiply" (Gen. 1:28, KJV).

In 1945 a group of eminent scientists convened in a strange location, the desert of New Mexico, to test the results of many long months of research. The success of their test could be of inestimable significance. It could be the key to rapidly terminating a long and costly war. The first testing of an atomic bomb was about to occur.

Atomic energy, whether in the form of nuclear warheads or plants producing valuable energy, has greatly shaped the progress of civilization since the dark days of Hiroshima.

The principle underlying the mechanism of an atomic bomb is simple. Fast moving neutrons are used to cause fission to occur within the bomb. As a neutron strikes the nucleus of a radioactive substance such as uranium, it causes it to split, forming two new, different nuclei, and in so doing to release three more neutrons. Each of these three neutrons now may strike a new nucleus and repeat the process. As each nucleus splits, energy is released. A chain reaction occurs, and the energy released takes the form of an explosion.

There is explosive power in multiplication, power that the disciple can see unleashed with the gospel of Jesus Christ.

The Principle of Multiplication

Multiplication is one of the foundational laws of the universe. Sheep, cattle, wildlife, trees, flowers, or bacteria—every growing thing operates on a principle of multiplication. Multiplication is God's way of doing things.

In Genesis 1:28 we read, "And God blessed them, and God said unto them, Be fruitful, and multiply, and replenish the earth, and subdue it; and have dominion over the fish of the sea, and over the fowl of the air, and over every living thing that moveth upon the earth" (KJV).

In this verse we find the first commandment that God ever gave to man, a commandment to multiply. This is about the only commandment that God has given us that we have ever been able to keep. Man has certainly multiplied upon the face of the earth.

Numerically, it works out as simply as this: If parents have two children they maintain the status quo; there is no net growth in the population. When parents have three or more children, then the population begins to multiply. The more children, the faster the multiplication process.

There is a certain cost involved in multiplication. Every parent knows that reproduction is costly. The more children you have, the more it costs to raise them. There are more interpersonal relationships to cope with in the family unit. There are more decisions to be made, greater chance for disease to strike a member of the family. There is a greater chance for heartache or disappointment in one form or another. Certainly more children take more time.

For a salmon, the cost of multiplication is death. A salmon swims upstream, lays its eggs in the sand, and then dies.

Grain also dies to reproduce. Jesus said, "Verily, verily, I say unto you, Except a corn of wheat fall into the ground and die, it abideth alone, but if it die, it bringeth forth much fruit" (John 12:24, KJV).

Even in the development of the atomic bomb, a cost was involved. In addition to the tremendous cost in terms of money and other resources, there was the "cost" to the atom itself. It had to be split and broken in order to produce its effect.

The cost involved in multiplication can also be seen in the

fact that it is initially slower than the process of addition. This is particularly important as we apply it to fulfilling the Great Commission. Let's say for example that a gifted evangelist is able to lead 1,000 people to Christ every day. Each year he will have reached 365,000 people, a phenomenal ministry indeed.

Let's compare him with a disciple who leads not *1,000 people a day* to Christ, but only *one person a year*. At the end of one year, the disciple has one convert; the evangelist, 365,000. But suppose the disciple has not only led his man to Christ, but has also discipled him. He has prayed with him, taught him how to feed himself from the Word of God, gotten him into fellowship with like-minded believers, taken him out on evangelism and showed him how to present the gospel to other people. At the end of that first year, this new convert is able to lead another man to Christ and follow him up as he himself has been followed up.

At the start of the second year, the disciple has doubled his ministry—the one has become two. During the second year, each man goes out and leads not 1,000 people per day to Christ, but one person per year. At the end of the second year, we have four people. You can see how slow our process is. But note, too, that we do not have only converts, but disciples who are able to reproduce themselves. At this rate of doubling every year, the disciple, leading one man per year to Christ, will overtake the evangelist numerically somewhere in the nineteenth year. From then on, the disciple and his multiplying ministry will be propagating faster than the combined ministry of dozens of gifted evangelists.

This is not to say that there is no need for the ministry of an evangelist, but that an evangelist by himself can never complete the task of reaching a lost and dying world.

It's like the dad who offered his two sons the choice of either taking one dollar a week for fifty-two weeks or one cent the first week, and the amount doubled every week for fifty-two weeks. One son took the dollar. The other son said, "Well, Dad, I will try the penny to see what will happen." We all know who wins: the son who takes the one penny and has it doubled each week. The degree to which he wins is absolutely astounding. By the end of the year, the son who began with the penny will have enough money to pay the United States national debt and still have plenty left over for himself!

God wants the same principles that are at work in the physical realm to be applied in the spiritual realm. The reason the church of Jesus Christ finds it so difficult to stay on top of the Great Commission is that the population of the world is multiplying while the church is merely adding. Addition can never keep pace with multiplication.

Some time ago there was a display at the Museum of Science and Industry in Chicago. It featured a checkerboard with 1 grain of wheat on the first square, 2 on the second, 4 on the third, then 8, 16, 32, 64, 128, etc. Somewhere down the board, there were so many grains of wheat on the square that some were spilling over into neighboring squares—so here the demonstration stopped. Above the checkerboard display was a question, "At this rate of doubling every square, how much grain would you have on the checkerboard by the time you reached the 64th square?"

To find the answer to this riddle, you punched a button on the console in front of you, and the answer flashed on a little screen above the board: "Enough to cover the entire subcontinent of India 50 feet deep."

Multiplication may be costly and, in the initial stages, much slower than addition, but in the long run, it is the most effective way of accomplishing Christ's Great Commission . . . and the only way.

Quality Is the Key to Multiplication

The key to success in the multiplying process is training the disciple in depth. Each time one person fails to "reproduce spiritually," you cut your results in half.

One of Adolf Hitler's objectives was the destruction of the Jewish race, but as determined as his endeavor was, he failed. The multiplication process had gone on for too long by the time he appeared on the scene. If, on the other hand, he could have been with Abraham on Mount Moriah, and taken that knife and plunged it into Isaac, he would have destroyed the entire Jewish race with one blow.

Today, nuclear reaction is used for producing energy. This use will grow increasingly during the coming years. The nuclear reaction is controlled by introducing a series of graphite rods into the reaction chamber. This slows down the multiplication process, preventing an explosion. As the church of Jesus Christ seeks to "explode" through multiplication, Satan is constantly trying to insert his "rods" to slow us down. One way Satan does this is indicated by Jesus Christ: "And the cares of this world, and the deceitfulness of riches, and the lusts of other things entering in, choke the Word, and it becometh unfruitful" (Mark 4:19, KJV).

Note what the apostle Paul says to Timothy, his son in the faith, "And the things that thou hast heard of me among many witnesses, the same commit thou to faithful men, who shall be able to teach others also" (2 Tim. 2:2, KJV). Four generations are clearly seen in Paul, Timothy, faithful men, and others also. Multiplication is assured only when there is proper training of faithful people who can carry the training process into succeeding generations.

It is easy to see that the training process needed to ensure multiplication is slow and costly. It takes a tremendous amount of time. And whenever you endeavor to insert a shortcut, you jeopardize the whole process. That is why the ministry of multiplying disciples has never been popular. Everybody likes the results it produces, but few are willing to pay the price to obtain the results.

A friend of mine and I were talking about a discipling ministry, and he said, "I am in the process of discipling fifty men right now." At that point I realized that he and I were talking about two entirely different things, for it is impossible to train fifty people at the same time. Disciples cannot be mass-produced.

While on earth, our Lord Jesus Christ was God in the form

of man. He was endowed with every spiritual gift, He did not have any of our weaknesses or failings, nor did He have the heavy responsibilities of being married or running a business; His time was devoted completely to the ministry. And yet, with all of these advantages, He felt that He could effectively train only twelve; and even out of those twelve, to really major in three. If twelve was the number our Lord decided on, I doubt if we, with all our limitations, can plan to effectively disciple fifty at one time.

In Paul's second letter to the Corinthians, he explains why he has embarked on a certain course of action by saying, "Furthermore, when I came to Troas to preach Christ's gospel, and a door was opened unto me of the Lord, I had no rest in my spirit, because I found not Titus my brother; but taking my leave of them, I went from thence into Macedonia" (2 Cor. 2:12-13, KJV).

When Paul came to Troas, not only did the Lord provide an opportunity to preach the gospel, but also people who were ready to listen. But Paul had a problem—he did not know the whereabouts of his co-laborer Titus. Because of this, he turned down the opportunity to reach the whole city of Troas and left in search of his brother Titus.

We would tend to think he made the wrong decision because he was allowing sentiment to rule his judgment. But perhaps finding Titus was more important than preaching to the whole city of Troas just then. Why? Because if Paul reached Titus and trained him, he would double the effectiveness of his ministry, and together they could turn around and reach two such cities as Troas instead of just one.

The importance of the individual in the process of multiplication can also be seen in Acts 8. Philip (believed to be one of the deacons chosen earlier, Acts 6) went to the city of Samaria and preached the gospel. "And the people with one accord gave heed unto those things which Philip spake, hearing and seeing the miracles which he did" (v. 6, KJV). The ministry was so successful that some of the leaders from Jerusalem came up to witness it and give it their blessing.

Right in the middle of this great evangelistic effort, the Spirit of God called Philip and sent him down to the Gaza desert to talk to one man—an Ethiopian eunuch (vv. 26-27). If Philip could multiply his ministry through the eunuch, then possibly this Ethiopian could become the key to reaching all of Ethiopia.

The discipling ministry lacks the glamour and excitement of the platform or large meeting type of ministry. But we can hardly overemphasize the importance of investing in the right kind of person, one of vision and discipline, totally committed to Jesus Christ, willing to pay any price to have the will of God fulfilled in his life. Sticking with a person and helping him to overcome the obstacles involved in becoming a disciple is a long and arduous task.

So often I have heard the excuse, "I just don't have the gift to do this kind of ministry." Or, "God just hasn't called me to this kind of ministry." The Great Commission given to us in Matthew 28:19-20 says, "Go therefore, and teach [make disciples of] all nations." It takes a disciple maker to make disciples. Historically the church has believed that the Great Commission was not given to a select few people, but to all believers. If this is true, then all believers can be disciple makers. Or, to put it another way, being involved in disciple-making transcends gifts and calling. Irrespective of our gifts or our calling, all men and women should be disciple makers.

Everyone has the gifts necessary to be a disciple maker. You may be a teacher, or a housewife, or an engineer, but irrespective of your vocation, you are also to be a disciple maker. If you are not a disciple maker, then I would suggest that you do the same thing that Timothy did with Paul, or that Peter, James, and John did with the Lord Jesus. Make yourself available to a disciple maker who can help you to become a disciple maker. Latch on to them. Learn from them the "how to" involved in developing those qualities needed to spiritually reproduce yourself in the lives of others.

Every Christian should ask himself two questions: "Who is

my Paul? Who is the person I am learning from, who is helping me to become a multiplying disciple maker?" And secondly, "Where is my Timothy? Where is the person I am in turn helping to become a multiplying disciple maker?"

Biblical Illustrations of Multiplication

Twelve sons were born to the patriarch Jacob. The Bible tells us that they multiplied and filled the land of Egypt. "And the children of Israel were fruitful, and increased abundantly, and *multiplied,* and waxed exceedingly mighty; and the land was filled with them" (Exod. 1:7, KJV). Jesus, likewise, chose twelve men to become His "spiritual children." He invested three years of His life in them and told them to become fruitful, to multiply, and to spread the Gospel to every creature. You and I are Christians now because twelve men caught Jesus' vision and did as He commanded. Spiritual reproduction works!

Paul's desire on his second missionary journey was to preach the gospel throughout Asia. Acts 16:6-11 tells us that the Holy Spirit checked his attempt and finally boxed him into the city of Troas. There Paul received the vision to go to Macedonia and preach the gospel. So, being forbidden of the Holy Spirit to preach the gospel in Asia, Paul and his team left and went to what is now Europe.

Now notice what happens on Paul's third missionary journey, as recorded in Acts 19. Paul is back in Asia once again, this time in the city of Ephesus. Verses 8-10 say: "And he went into the synagogue, and spake boldly for the space of three months, disputing and persuading the things concerning the kingdom of God. But when divers were hardened, and believed not, but spake evil of that way before the multitude, he departed from them, and separated the disciples, disputing daily in the school of one Tyrannus. And this continued by the space of two years; so that all they which dwelt in Asia heard the word of the Lord Jesus, both Jews and Greeks" (KJV).

Here is a beautiful illustration of spiritual multiplication. Because of Paul's discipling ministry in the school of Tyrannus, everyone in the province of Asia heard the word of the Lord Jesus. And just to make the point clear, Luke adds, "both Jews and Greeks."

Multiplying disciples is the New Testament vision and method for getting the job done. We have not taken time in this chapter to do an exhaustive study on the principle of multiplication from the Scriptures, but this might be a topical study you would like to do on your own. You will certainly find it rewarding.

Discipleship is not the ministry of any one particular organization or church. It is God's ministry. It has been on His heart from the beginning of time. Just as He set up the physical propagation of the human race on a multiplying basis, He has likewise set up the spiritual propagation of the human race on a multiplying basis. But, because of the spiritual battle involved, many would-be disciples disqualify themselves. God's cry to the prophet Ezekiel is His cry today: "And I sought for a man among them, that should make up the hedge, and stand in the gap before Me for the land that I should not destroy it: but I found none" (Ezek. 22:30, KJV). Have you heard His cry? Will you be that person? Will you be God's disciple maker?

7

Disciple Making
and the Church

BILLIE HANKS, JR.

Can discipling be done successfully in the local church, or is it something that only parachurch groups can do well? Billie Hanks's whole ministry at present is tied to his firm conviction that disciple making can be carried on successfully in the local church. Furthermore, pastors and key lay leaders can be trained to have a multiplying ministry of discipleship in their churches. Hanks firmly believes that the potential of multiplication evangelism and the dynamic of the one-on-one discipling relationship "are rooted historically in the local church."

The process has simply been lost and is only now being rediscovered. Billie's ministry is one of multiplying that rediscovery in churches and denominations in North America and on the mission fields of the world.

This chapter introduces us to a specific methodology that has worked extremely well in the hundreds of churches that have done what their leaders were trained to do. The details and specific how-to's of this methodology are available in the Christian Discipleship Seminars held throughout the United States.

(Information on when and where the seminars are scheduled is available from the International Evangelism Association, P.O. Box 6883, Fort Worth, Texas 76115. IEA may also be contacted about organizing a seminar for your area.)

7

Disciple Making and the Church

BILLIE HANKS, JR.

"'Come and follow me,' Jesus said, 'and I will make you fishers of men'" (Matt. 4:19).

The book to this point has exposed us to the vision of discipleship, its biblical basis, and the concept and methodology of evangelistic multiplication. It is hoped that God has used these last six chapters to instill in you a profound desire to implement these concepts in both your church and your personal life.

This transition chapter will move us away from philosophy of ministry into the practical questions related to developing a multiplication ministry in our individual churches. Multiplication evangelism has been presented as the first major principle of this book. The following chapters will deal with the second basic principle, which has to do with the roles of teaching and training in the process of disciple making.

Distinguishing Teaching From Training

Many of the church's evangelistic failures of the past have resulted from attempting to impart through *teaching* those skills which were designed by God to be instilled in one's spiritual life through *training*. Historically, in the educational process knowledge has been transferred through these two different yet complementary forms of instruction: teaching and training.

Teaching requires the transmission of ideas and concepts. A gifted teacher can hold the attention of tens, hundreds, or even thousands. Typically, words are used to convey his thoughts, and he needs little else to get his point across. Our Lord was a master teacher; His illustrations and parables are beyond equal. The size of the groups He spoke to had no bearing on His ability to clearly express the truth. He was comfortable with twelve or a gathering of well over five thousand. His teaching of the Sermon on the Mount points up that any size groups can be taught spiritual truths as long as they *can* hear and *want* to hear what is being said (Matt. 5:1-2).

This is not true with training, however. *Training requires the transmission of learned skills.* The term that best communicates this concept in many cultures is *apprenticeship.* Because observation and practical experience are needed for effective training to occur, one-on-one relationships are universally used as the accepted apprenticing format.

Let me use aviation to illustrate the difference between teaching and training. One summer I was flying in a small airplane with a highly experienced pilot instructor. Having spent little time in small aircraft, I became a bit concerned as we crossed the tall mountains of New Mexico: What would happen if the pilot had a heart attack while we were flying at eight thousand feet? I suggested that he take a few minutes and instruct me on the basics of crash-landing an airplane.

As we talked, he said, "Billie, do you know why I am so sold on personal disciple making?"

"No, but I would like to," I replied.

"When you go to flight school," he said, "and you are 'discipled' in how to fly an aircraft, your basic instruction is usually conducted on the ground and in a small group. In that setting you learn the concepts of aerodynamics; but later on, after ground instruction, all pilot training is done in a plane one-on-one. Every pilot in the air today has been individually *apprenticed* to fly. It works in aeronautics, and it works in the Christian life."

In Jesus' ministry of instruction, He was sometimes with His disciples in a group, and at other times with them individually. He discipled them on both levels, and they ultimately became effective fishers of men.

The same principle holds true in the practice of medicine. Surgeons who perform the most delicate surgery are required to have the longest and most personalized periods of internship training. In general, the more critical the consequence of failure, the greater the need for thorough individual instruction.

If for no other reason than this, training in evangelism, which involves eternity, must demand our very best and most committed effort. The Lord's emphasis on training emerged early in His ministry. "As Jesus was walking beside the Sea of Galilee, he saw two brothers, Simon called Peter and his brother Andrew. They were casting a net into the lake, for they were fishermen. 'Come, follow me,' Jesus said, 'and I will make you fishers of men.' At once they left their nets and followed him" (Matt. 4:18-20). Their on-the-job training had begun.

One summer as I was attempting to trout fish while on vacation in Colorado, I experienced a vivid illustration of apprenticeship. Although I was trying hard, the fish were not cooperating. Experiencing no success, I realized I needed some expert help.

I started looking for an instructor—someone who could apprentice me in fishing. I discovered that one of my friends was an experienced fly fisherman, and he was willing to train me in the art. He spent a brief time explaining the ins and outs of fishing and the difference between a dry fly and a wet fly. This was my teaching period. I was learning the theory of fishing.

Then he said, "Let's take one of these flies, attach it to a line, and go out in the front yard, where we can actually practice casting." I was now moving from teaching to training, by applying the knowledge I had gained.

He placed his hands next to mine on the rod, and for several minutes we cast the little fly toward a small yellow daisy until I could land the fly near the daisy every time. He then went into his garage and brought out some large wading hip boots. I put them on, and he had me walk around his yard casting the fly.

Having given me the on-shore instruction, my trainer said, "Now you are ready for the real thing."

I thought he would take me to a little stream like the one in which I had been fishing. To my surprise, however, he took me to a wide, rushing mountain stream where he knew the fish to be plentiful.

I learned something important through this experience. In our evangelism many of us don't reach people simply because we are fishing in the wrong streams. We are more concerned about the beauty and convenience of our fishing spots than the ultimate success of our mission.

My instructor took me to the right place, but the water was fast and in places, deep. I remember looking into my rubber waders and realizing how much water they could hold if I fell.

The instructor said, "Just follow me."

He stepped out into the water, and it became deep quickly, so he turned around and said something very practical. "Billie, don't ever commit your weight to a rock until you test it. Put your foot on it and then rock your foot to see if it will roll under the force of the water. Next, slide your foot over the surface of the rock to check for moss that would cause you to slip. When you cast, watch out for those low hanging tree limbs to the right. Notice the way I cast down under them."

I followed his example to the letter and quickly caught several nice rainbow trout. That was a tremendous improvement over my previous experience. What made the difference? First, I was under the guidance of an outstanding teacher and trainer who was an experienced fisherman. Second, I was taught in the basic concepts of fishing before getting into the water. Third, he trained me in how to fish by example; I was apprenticed as I followed him in the stream. Through his guidance I was using the right fly for the right stream at the right time of day.

Quality discipling emphasizes a balanced combination of the two principal methods of instruction: that which can be learned through *teaching* and that which can be learned through *training*. One method deals with ideas, the other with skills.

The Principle Applied in Church Ministries

Unfortunately, most churches merely *teach* new Christians without giving them the benefit of apprenticeship-type *training*. How can this be changed?

Some years ago I received a phone call from the Southern Baptist Director of Evangelism for about a thousand churches in California. He was struggling with this same question. After much prayer and months of work, we decided to begin a pilot project attempting to implement lay apprenticeship training for the purpose of multiplication evangelism.

Seventy selected churches originally took part in this exciting endeavor. By the end of five years, certified trainers from 238 churches were involved in what was then North America's largest and longest pilot effort in planned local-church participation in one-on-one disciple making.

The five-year experiment helped us to understand and validate the two major concepts of discipleship that have been presented in this book. However, many of the specific methods of applying these concepts proved to be different from what we had anticipated at the beginning. We learned five valuable lessons in methodology.

Assigned Training Relationships. At our request, participating pastors instructed the laymen whom they had trained simply to follow God's leading in finding their own Timothys[1] as new Christians entered the fellowship of the church. This sounded spiritual and met with approval in the churches. However, as time passed, it became evident that the new converts did not

---

[1]"Timothy" and "Timothette" are terms used to describe new Christians who are being discipled by trained lay people, who are called "Pauls" and "Paulettes" in Christian Discipleship Seminars.

know enough to seek out more mature Christians to disciple them. The more-trained laypeople were typically timid about seeking new converts to disciple. In other words, the non-directive, unstructured approach to linking the new convert to a more mature believer proved impractical.

We discovered that a layperson was needed in each church for the purpose of coordinating the assignment of new Christians to mature disciple makers. That simple insight vastly increased the effectiveness of the discipling process in the churches.

Curriculum. Another major discovery stemmed from the concern that one-on-one training could degenerate from a life-to-life relationship to the mere transfer of knowledge from one notebook to another. Acknowledging this possibility, we studiously avoided developing a written guide for these laypersons to use in training a Timothy. This was a serious mistake.

The first trained laypeople encountered problems because they were unable to organize what they had learned in order to share it in a logical sequence. They now had fresh concepts and new disciplines, but no curriculum to guide them in helping train their Timothys.

Therefore we developed charts to guide the Pauls in their week-by-week meetings with their Timothys. With the addition of this tool, a major fear was eliminated for the participating lay trainers. With the aid of the new curriculum guides for one-on-one training, hundreds of additional laypeople began to train their Timothys effectively.

Accountability. We gained a third valuable insight when we learned that dedicated people respond to a realistic call to spiritual accountability. A quality-conscious pastor began to require a covenant on the part of the lay leaders being trained to serve as Pauls. On the basis of his obvious success, other pastors as well began making the following five requirements of their potential church disciple makers:

As an expression of my personal commitment to Jesus Christ, I covenant with the Lord, my pastor, and my fellow believers—

- To participate in each of the fifteen discipleship group sessions unless providentially hindered.
- To carry out each Spiritual Growth Assignment to the best of my ability.
- To personally apprentice a new or younger Christian at the conclusion of the group discipleship instruction.
- To pray for the opportunity to witness at least once each day during the discipleship group instruction.
- To seek to maintain a teachable spirit as unto Christ.

Date _____ Signature _____

With this added accountability factor, the disciple-making process in the church was significantly strengthened.

Division of the Training. The fourth major observation dealt with the needs of the new converts. We discovered that the first eight to ten weeks of their pilgrimage in Christianity must be considered as follow-up rather than full-fledged apprenticeship training. In the earlier stage—which will be developed by Gary Kuhne in chapters 8 and 9—we will see the specific needs of new converts. In chapter 10, William Shell and LeRoy Eims will deal with the more advanced process of apprenticeship.

Evaluation and Report. The fifth lesson had to do with encouraging the trainers (the Pauls and Paulettes). We found they needed regular evaluation and report sessions on the progress of their ministries. After experimenting with numerous schedules, it became clear that these sessions must be conducted weekly or at least twice a month. The sessions had to remain lay-centered and focus on testimonies of evangelism and the continued personal growth of the trainees. Ample time had to be provided for honest discussion concerning the needs of the Timothys being trained.

The spontaneous enthusiasm and mutual accountability generated by this ongoing process is the strength of a church's disciple-making effort.

After training about ten thousand laypeople over a five-year period, the 238 participating churches were studied as a seminary sabbatical project. The results came slowly as we learned valuable lessons, but in the fifth year the churches experienced an encouraging 18 percent increase in new converts as the result of their evangelism.[2]

Some Observations on the Disciple Making Process

If any single factor has hampered pastors and staff members in establishing a ministry of multiplication through apprenticeship training, it is their concern over the amount of time required for training an individual. If you are facing this problem, let me offer a liberating and encouraging solution.

The concepts of one-on-one training can be *taught* to a small group of your most spiritually mature laypeople. Your teaching ministry can be carried out over a period of several months, even though you are unable to *train* them individually. It has been our experience that mature laypeople are the product of a large number of *unstructured* teaching and training relationships that have occurred as a result of the various ministries of the church. Therefore, even though they may not receive one-on-one training from a pastor, they are potentially prepared to make disciples if given the benefit of specific instruction and guidance in that direction. Many of these laypeople already possess a high percentage of the knowledge needed to apprentice a new convert. The lacking ingredients are simply vision, organization, and access to the proper tools.

This means that as a staff member you can have two levels of ministry. You can teach the philosophy of discipleship and explain its spiritual disciplines on a group level. Beyond that, however, you can personally apprentice one or two laypeople per year on a one-on-one basis. Hundreds of pastors are already experiencing the spiritual rewards and evangelistic results afforded by this simple and workable approach to disciple making in the church.

A second liberating concept can be described in this way:

---

[2]Statistical data compiled by Dr. Roy J. Fish, Professor of Evangelism, Southwestern Baptist Theological Seminary, Fort Worth, Texas.

The more mature the Timothy, the less structured the relationship. It has been my privilege to have been trained by seven men in my Christian life. Several of them have continued to invest their lives in my own. The relationship that started out in a structured manner when I was a young Christian has steadily progressed to close friendship with these men of God.

In a church setting, follow-up will typically last only a few weeks, while a quality apprenticing relationship may require a year or even more. After that, you may expect to see a continued colleagueship between the Pauls and the Timothys as the individual ministries of multiplication begin to grow.

We should expect results, but always with the awareness that we are growing an oak tree. Disciple making is a process that is steady, fulfilling, and effective. If impatience characterizes a pastor, he will tend to build his ministry around events at the expense of a long-range disciple-making process. Visualize a rope with several knots in it. Which is more important: the knots, or the rope that connects them? Balance is the key! It is good to have a variety of events in the life of a church, but these events—though meaningful at the time—lose their long-range effectiveness unless they are connected to one another by a strong, continuing multiplication and equipping process.

Another observation is the vital need to distinguish between teaching and training, as described earlier in this chapter. I talked with a pastor who had been meeting one-on-one with his key laypeople for five years. The expected fruit of discipleship was all there except evangelism. He wondered why. The rope must come first and then the knots.

Through our discussion I learned that he was teaching his laypeople without training them, even though they were meeting one-on-one. They never went witnessing together or ministered together as a team on the church field. All their activities were related to Bible study, Scripture memory, prayer, and character development. We must not assume that the skill of witnessing will spontaneously develop as a result of these other disciplines. Although these activities build depth and faith in the lives of believers, ultimately we must go out together and witness if we want our Timothys to become evangelizers.

One of the outstanding ministries that works on the apprenticeship principle of on-the-job training is Evangelism Explosion. We discovered that it works ideally with one-on-one follow-up and discipleship training. One emphasis provides instruction in threshold visits and direct evangelism; the other provides instruction in how to apprentice a convert for a lifestyle of spiritual growth and multiplication evangelism. It is as if God the Holy Spirit merged the two emphases in order to underscore the need for a full cycle of evangelism in the church.

A fourth exciting observation is the fact that even a *very small church* can begin the disciple-making process. My first pastorate was a church with only seven members, but in that rural community God gave me the opportunity to disciple a young turkey farmer who had a tremendous desire to grow in Christ. You only need one to start the process.

People of all ages can become disciple makers. A friend told me an exciting story about a seventy-eight-year-old woman in a wheelchair who was meeting with five women in her home, one each weekday. The training aspect of the disciple-making process, which she could not fully carry out because of her lack of mobility, was left to others.

Asked why she had never taught a Sunday school class, she replied, "I am timid before a group, but I like helping one person at a time." She added that she wished someone had shown her the importance of personally teaching women years ago so she would not have wasted so much valuable time.

Age makes no difference, and being in a wheelchair need not hold anyone back. Some of the best discipling today is being accomplished by retirees who have much spiritual wisdom to share with a younger generation of believers.

The fifth observation has to do with the time period in which a Paul should be assigned to work with a Timothy. The minister of discipleship of a large church in Albuquerque, New Mexico, shared some statistics with me. Careful research on four hundred converts above the age of fifteen confirmed our findings concerning the importance of immediate follow-up. It was discovered that of those Timothys who met together with a Paul on the first week after joining the church, 90 percent completed the ten weeks of basic follow-up instruction. Of those who did not get started until the second week, 70 percent completed the ten weeks. Of those who did not begin until the third week, only 30 percent completed their training, and serious attrition had already begun!

Summary

The belief that one-on-one discipleship training cannot be accomplished in a local church has been laid to rest. It is apparent that the explosive power of multiplication evangelism and the practicality of personal apprenticeship are rooted historically in the local church.

When these two New Testament principles are replanted in the church, where they flourished in the first century, the Great Commission will again be carried out with the tremendous force and blessing that were experienced in those amazing decades of evangelism.

The following chapters deal specifically with how to make that happen. They tell us where to begin and how to build for the future.

8

Follow-up—
An Overview

GARY W. KUHNE

The first step toward building disciples in our churches or in our ministry begins with follow-up. Brand new Christians or "old" untaught Christians need to be followed up carefully if they are to achieve the potential for service that God has planned (see Eph. 2:10). Gary W. Kuhne defines follow-up as "the spiritual work of grounding a new believer in the faith." His years of practical experience with Campus and Lay Mobilization in Erie, Pennsylvania, in an evangelistic, follow-up, and discipling ministry qualify him to speak with authority on this subject. He also served with Campus Crusade for Christ.

Gary Kuhne is a graduate of the Pennsylvania State University and at present is pastor of Fellowship Baptist Church in North East, Pennsylvania.

This chapter, excerpted from his *Dynamics of Personal Follow-up* (Zondervan, 1976), deals specifically and practically with the many facets of personal follow-up. Careful study of his material and practical suggestions should enable us not only to commit ourselves to follow-up in our churches, but to begin doing it successfully in our ministry.

8

Follow-up—
An Overview

GARY W. KUHNE

"Strengthening the disciples" (Acts 14:22).

For many of you who read this book, personal follow-up may be a new concept. It is perhaps a work you have heard about—but you have never actively participated in such a ministry. Don't be ashamed of this. Personal follow-up is simply a ministry that has been neglected by Christian leaders. My experience has shown that the vast majority of people with whom I counsel are not personally involved in following up new Christians.

Studies have shown that less than one percent of evangelical church members are involved in personal follow-up. For many years I thought the lack of personal evangelism was one of the greatest problems facing the church. I have not changed my mind as to the seriousness of this problem. But I now believe the lack of effective follow-up being done in the local church today constitutes an even more dangerous problem for the church at large. Perhaps a few examples from my personal experience will show you the reason for my burden in this area.

One of my first exposures to evangelistic outreach began optimistically. A student at Penn State University, I had been a Christian for nearly two years. While in high school, before becoming a Christian, I had been the president of the youth group in my home church, and now I felt a strong burden for the youth currently in that group. I sought to find a way to make the gospel clear to them. The opportunity presented itself when the youth leader wrote me and requested that I come and lead a weekend retreat. This was a clear answer to prayer, and with the help of several friends, I set about planning the retreat.

The retreat was finally held and God's Spirit moved in a beautiful way. Only one person out of the entire youth group rejected the gospel invitation. I went back to college rejoicing in the Lord. It wasn't long, however, before I began to have serious doubts about the success of the weekend. The youth leader wrote me and told me about problems arising in the group. Several of those who made commitments were no longer attending. As time went on, all but a few apparently forgot their commitments. I felt helpless to do something about the problem. At that time I did not see the significant role personal follow-up could have played in conserving the fruit of the retreat. This experience jolted me into discovering how to conserve the fruit of evangelism.

Another situation impressed on me the need for effective personal follow-up. This was an evangelistic film outreach in which I was involved. My role was to act as the head counselor, guiding the work of volunteers who counseled with those who came forward in response to the invitation given after the film. The training the counselors received was completely evangelistic in nature and no attention was given to helping the new believer grow in his new life in Christ (I admit this to my shame). The response in the week of film showings was remarkable. Nearly one thousand people came forward to seek the answer to their needs and problems. After approximately six months, I felt burdened to see what lasting result was evident from our ministry. Although communication was a limiting factor, it was still clear there was little lasting fruit from that project. I could account for fewer than two dozen out of the thousand inquirers who still were going on in their decision. I am not relating this to criticize film evangelism; in fact I feel it is a very effective way to communicate the gospel. I am attempting to show that unless there is a strong emphasis on personal follow-up of decisions, there will be little lasting fruit to show for our efforts.

How much difference can an effective personal follow-up program make in the conservation of fruit in evangelistic outreach? Let me cite another example. An evangelistic church with whose ministry I am acquainted reveals an interesting insight into the role of follow-up in fruit conservation. Examining the church records over the past ten years revealed that approximately six hundred decisions for Christ were made in that time. These decisions resulted from a variety of programs, i.e., youth retreats, evangelism weeks, evangelistic services, personal evangelism, etc. The profession of faith statistics, taken from an analysis of membership increase over the same time period, numbered less than one hundred. Thus it would seem that only one out of six decisions was actually conserved. Although this figure does not take into account those who were already members when saved or those who went on in the Lord and joined some other body, it is safe to say that accurate information concerning these other people would not significantly alter the conservation figure of one out of six.

The reason I chose this church as an example is that the leadership in this church decided they could no longer be content with such a low conservation rate. A number of their people received training in personal follow-up and determined to use their training with every person who would respond to the invitation in their church. Soon after that they had an evangelistic week at their church and for the first time sought to follow up on all who responded. After six months the fruit conservation rate was five out of six. Personal follow-up indeed made a significant difference.

My experience over the past several years could multiply these examples of the limitations of evangelism without personal follow-up. Well-planned personal follow-up of new believers could, I am convinced, revolutionize the traditional growth rates of local churches. I believe we can no longer explain away those who don't continue to grow in Christ as being "seeds in bad soil" (see the parable of the sower and the seed in Matt. 13). Undoubtedly some of those who don't continue to grow in the Lord are the products of "bad soil," yet I see no implication in the text to support a fruit conservation rate of one out of six. Personal experience has shown a much higher rate resulting from effective personal follow-up of new believers. I believe the need is so urgent we can no longer be complacent about so few lasting results in evangelism.

Definition of Follow-up

Since this is a book about personal follow-up, it would be good at the outset to define clearly the meaning of this phrase. Because I am unfamiliar with the background of every reader, and the meanings he or she applies to terms, it will be necessary for us to establish some common ground in the area of definitions. For the purpose of this book, follow-up is defined as follows:

> *Follow-up* is the spiritual work of grounding a new believer in the faith.

This is a generally accepted definition by most Christians I have consulted. The following verses are an example of the emphasis the Bible places on this work of building new believers in the faith.

> We proclaim him, admonishing and teaching everyone with all wisdom, so that we may present everyone perfect in Christ. To this end I labor, struggling with all the energy he so powerfully works in me (Col. 1:28-29).

> They preached the good news in that city and won a large number of disciples. Then they returned to Lystra, Iconium and Antioch, strengthening the disciples and encouraging them to remain true to the faith (Acts 14:21-22).

In light of the biblical emphasis on follow-up, the serious Christian has no choice but to do it. The only question that requires discussion is how follow-up can be accomplished most effectively.

An explanation of the basic definition already given is necessary to clarify the content of this term. The spiritual work of grounding a new believer in the faith is going to be the product of both training and teaching. There are certain basic spiritual truths a new Christian must know and apply to become rooted and really begin to grow in Christ. The following is a list of five basic areas of spiritual truth involved in an effective follow-up program:

1. Helping the new believer receive assurance of salvation and acceptance with God.
2. Helping the new believer develop a consistent devotional life.
3. Helping the new believer understand the basics of abundant Christian living.
4. Helping the new believer become integrated into the life of a local church.
5. Helping the new believer learn to share his faith with others.

Another helpful explanation of follow-up would be that it is the assuming of a parent-child relationship with a new believer. This is in the spiritual realm, of course. The Bible describes the new believer as a spiritual baby (John 3:3; 1 Cor. 3:1; 1 Peter 2:2; 1 John 2:12-14). This description is an accurate one. Love, protection, food, and training are vital spiritual needs that correspond to the physical needs of a baby. As in the physical realm, a new Christian needs a spiritual parent who will watch over him and help provide these necessities during the early stages of his Christian development.

The work of follow-up in a new Christian's life might be better understood by examining the three basic forms it takes: Sunday school group, personal study, and personal follow-up. Group follow-up is that nurturing of the new believer accomplished by the local church or fellowship group. This kind of follow-up takes the form of structured instruction in the basics of doctrine through the use of a new believers' class, Sunday school, or similar program. It also includes the development of committed relationships between the new Christian and the

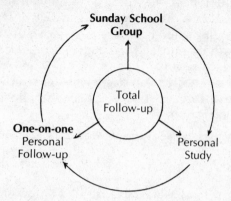

Fig. 1. Elements of a Total Follow-up Program

body of believers with whom he associates. The second form, personal study, includes those activities the new Christian engages in on his own. This would include such things as reading books and literature and personal Bible study. On both the group and personal study levels of follow-up there is quite a bit of information available to the average pastor and layman to help implement these aspects of a total follow-up ministry. Unfortunately in the past the same could not be said for the third form, personal follow-up, which is the major emphasis of this book and can be defined as follows:

> *Personal follow-up* is the assuming of a one-to-one relationship by a mature believer with a new Christian for the purpose of aiding the new Christian's nurture and growth.

This type of follow-up, by far the most effective, as I will seek to show, is the most neglected form among Christians today.

My experience has shown two major causes for failure in personal follow-up. First, many Christians are unclear as to what needs to be done to help ground a new believer in the faith. In some cases, where the Christian has the general knowledge of *what* to say, he is unsure of *how* to say it. This accounts for much ineffectiveness. Secondly, many Christians are unwilling to give the time effective personal follow-up requires. As we will examine later in this book, the time requirements of personal work are considerable. Although there are other reasons for the lack of personal follow-up work by Christians, I will focus upon these two.

Importance of Personal Follow-up

Having clearly dealt with what follow-up is, the question now before us is: Why is personal follow-up important? That the Bible commands us to follow up new believers has already been shown. But since the work of follow-up takes three forms, I would like to propose four reasons why you should not be content to simply abdicate your personal responsibility in follow-up to the group, or the initiative of the new believer. Rather you should consider personal follow-up a priority.

1. *The Vulnerability of a New Christian.* A new Christian is more easily deceived by Satan than a more mature Christian. In fact, a new believer is more vulnerable in the fight against Satan's temptations than at any other time of his life. It is common for a new Christian to experience doubt regarding the validity of his decision for Christ. He needs the protection that a more mature believer can help to give him. Victory against Satan's deceptions is only to be found in the truths of God's Word. Christ taught us this by using the Bible to answer Satan's temptations in the wilderness (Matt. 4:1-11; Mark 1:12-13; Luke 4:1-13). Knowing little of the Word of God makes a new Christian quite defenseless. This vulnerability is a strong argument for involvement in personal follow-up.

2. *The New Christian's Potential for Change.* A second important reason for personal follow-up involves the new Christian's rate of growth. A new Christian is at a pivotal point in his life. For the first time, he has the potential for real change in his life style. The direction and guidance offered through personal follow-up greatly increase both the chance and speed of this transformation. Young person or adult, personal follow-up greatly speeds one's growth in Christ. A mature Christian working in such a close relationship with a new

Christian is able to detect the areas in his life that need the most urgent change. He is also able to assist in the application of pertinent biblical truth. Without this personal guidance, many new Christians are not able to take full advantage of this crucial period of their lives and do not grow in Christ as rapidly as they could.

A closely related problem is the developing of wrong life patterns in the new Christian who is unsupervised in his growth. These patterns not only hinder his growth, but present unnecessary sin problems that need to be undone in the future before real, lasting growth can take place. This process of change is described in Scripture as a "putting off" of the old man and a "putting on" of the new man. Ephesians 4 and Colossians 3 explain this concept more completely. The truth of these passages should do much to motivate us for the work of personal follow-up.

3. *Disciples Are Produced Most Effectively Through Personal Follow-up.* A third important reason for doing personal follow-up involves the development of disciples. Personal follow-up greatly increases the speed and probability of discipleship development in a new believer's life. An important and basic goal of your ministry in this area is the development of disciples. It is important that the term *disciple* be clearly defined in your mind. My experience has proven that there are almost as many definitions of this term as there are people. For the purpose of this book, a disciple is defined as follows:

> A *disciple* is a Christian who is growing in conformity to Christ, is achieving fruit in evangelism, and is working in follow-up to conserve his fruit.

Discipleship training should be a major goal in a total program of personal follow-up. When I use the term *personal follow-up*, I am using it in both a limited and an expanded sense. In the limited sense, I am referring to the initial work of grounding a new believer in the faith. In the expanded sense, I am using the phrase to refer to the entire relationship a mature Christian has with a new Christian over a period of time to help the new Christian achieve maturity. To prevent misunderstanding, I define *discipleship training* as follows:

> *Discipleship training* is the spiritual work of developing spiritual maturity and spiritual reproductiveness in the life of a Christian.

Effective personal follow-up of a new Christian will go far toward conserving more of the fruit of evangelism, but will not in itself speed the fulfillment of the Great Commission. Only an increasing labor force can accomplish this task. The development of spiritual reproductiveness in the new believer's life is the answer to this need. Stated differently, the new Christian must not only be taught to grow in Christ, but he must also be taught to witness and follow up others who respond to Christ. This alone will achieve a truly multiplying effectiveness in fulfilling the Great Commission. This fact brings us to the fourth reason for making the work of personal follow-up a priority in your life.

4. *Personal Follow-up Is the Most Effective Way of Achieving Spiritual Multiplication.* The degree to which you can encourage a new Christian to be fruit-producing has important implications for the fulfillment of the Great Commission. The previous section showed the truth of this statement. Your effectiveness in this work will determine whether you will be a spiritual "adder" or "multiplier." Will you only *lead people to Christ,* or will you also be responsible for *their leading others to Christ* (these who in turn will lead others to Christ)? Not only spiritual productiveness, but also spiritual *re*productiveness should be the focus of your personal follow-up ministry. To be a multiplier should be the goal of every Christian. A multiplier may be defined as follows:

> A *multiplier* is a disciple who is training his spiritual children to reproduce themselves.

In other words, a multiplier is a disciple who is able to produce other disciples. Only when this process occurs will we see true spiritual multiplication. I define multiplication as follows:

Multiplication is third-generation discipleship training.

To further explain, third-generation discipleship training is seeing someone you have personally discipled discipling another to disciple others. It is extremely important to understand the concept of spiritual multiplication, for it is the goal of this book to produce spiritually multiplying Christians.

Spiritual multiplication is a process that goes through four distinct phases. An explanation of these phases aids in the understanding of this concept.

Phase 1: Evangelizing. The first phase in spiritual multiplication occurs when we share our faith with other people. The command to witness was implied in the Great Commission: "Go ye therefore, and teach all nations, baptizing them in the name of the Father, and of the Son, and of the Holy Ghost: Teaching them to observe all things whatsoever I have commanded you" (Matt. 28:19-20). There can be no short-cut. It is essential that you share Christ with others. Although the *method* of evangelism may vary widely, the *message* cannot. As you share Christ in the power of the Holy Spirit, you will begin to see results, i.e., fruit. When an individual repents and receives Christ as his Savior and Lord, you begin a second phase of the multiplication process.

Phase 2: Personal Follow-up. Phase 2 of the multiplication process occurs when you personally start to follow up a new Christian. You begin to meet with him on a regular basis to give him the basic care and teaching he needs to grow in Christ. While in phase 1 all your ministry time was spent in witnessing, now in phase 2 you are beginning to devote a growing percentage of your time to the work of building the new Christian. You continue to share Christ even while you are involved in the work of personal follow-up. It is important not to neglect this work. Part of your work in follow-up involves challenging the new believer to a public identification with Christ and a proclaiming of the gospel, i.e., witnessing. When the new believer begins to do this you have, in effect, doubled your evangelistic outreach as the result of working with another believer to get him involved in witnessing.

It is important to remember that witnessing by itself does not go far enough to fulfill the Great Commission. At a certain point in time, either when a new Christian has grown sufficiently in Christ or when he leads someone else to Christ, a new phase must begin. You must start to train the new Christian to personally follow up someone else (ground them in the faith). This is what has been previously defined as discipleship training, or "discipling," for short. When you begin this distinct phase of personal ministry, you begin phase 3 of the multiplication process.

Phase 3: Discipling. Phase 3 begins when you start to *train* the Christian you are working with to personally follow up another new Christian. This is a distinct phase because now you are working with a new Christian to enable him not only to keep growing in Christ, but also to become effective in the work of personal follow-up. This not only adds people to the witnessing team, but it also adds them to the fruit-conservation team. Phase 3 is obviously a longer phase than phase 2 because it takes much longer to train a new Christian to do personal follow-up than to help him begin to grow in Christ. The work of phase 3 goes through three distinct levels:

1. Teaching him to follow up someone.
2. Teaching him to teach others to follow up someone.
3. Teaching him to teach others to teach others to follow up someone.

The goal is the multiplication of teachers. This is the truth Paul sought to relate to Timothy in "And the things you have heard me say in the presence of many witnesses (level 1) entrust to reliable men (level 2) who will also be qualified to teach others (level 3)."

Examine this phase more closely and you will find a great increase in the number of evangelistic contacts. This increase is the product of multiplication of laborers, not the product of increased witnessing on your part. An even more significant point that comes out if you examine phase 3: There are now more people to do follow-up. Now you are multiplying your effectiveness in outreach. It is also important to notice that as you go into discipleship training with someone, you will probably see more fruit and be forced to start follow-up all over again with someone else.

You probably have a question at this point: Why is there another phase for multiplication? Multiplication really begins when two factors are present:

1. A person has been discipled through level 3 (2 Tim. 2:2).
2. A person actually begins to take someone else through a discipling process.

Thus, multiplication must go beyond merely training and teaching, the goal of phase 3, to implementation. And this brings us to phase 4.

Phase 4: Multiplying. Phase 4 is the multiplying stage of the multiplication process. This is where 2 Timothy 2:2 has become a reality in your ministry. Phase 4 occurs when a person, followed-up and discipled by you, is following up and discipling others. This is the goal of your follow-up ministry and can be accomplished *no other way than through one-to-one involvement and training.* The fulfillment of the Great Commission is a reality only when 2 Timothy 2:2 becomes a reality. We must evangelize, follow up, train, and send if we are to see the world evangelized. If you only develop one truly multiplying disciple each year (not an unreasonable goal), examine what growth will take place for the gospel outreach as a product of your life over a six-year period. As a result of making a commitment to begin each day by praying for a natural opportunity to witness, let's assume that one evangelistic contact per week is made by each disciple:

Year One
  1. Begin year: 1 disciple (you)
  2. End year: 2 disciples (you, plus 1)
  3. Evangelistic contacts: 50 approximately

Year Two
  1. Begin year: 2 disciples

2. End Year: 4 disciples
3. Evangelistic contacts: 100 approximately

Year Three
1. Begin year: 4 disciples
2. End year: 8 disciples
3. Evangelistic contacts: 200 approximately

Year Four
1. Begin year: 8 disciples
2. End year: 16 disciples
3. Evangelistic contacts: 400 approximately

Year Five
1. Begin year: 16 disciples
2. End year: 32 disciples
3. Evangelistic contacts: 800 approximately

Year Six
1. Begin year: 32 disciples
2. End year: 64 disciples
3. Evangelistic contacts: 1,600 approximately

In a six-year period, if you only discipled 6 people, you will have caused the eventual development of 64 disciples and the evangelistic confrontation of 1,600 people per year. This is how the multiplication process works. If you continued the process for ten years, you would have personally discipled 10 people and witnessed to 50 a year—but you will have caused the development of 1,024 disciples and the annual confrontation with the gospel of approximately 25,000 people. This isn't just mathematical juggling but the logical outgrowth of faithful working for the Lord.

The most important "why" of personal follow-up is answered by a firm grasp of the vision of multiplication. My hope is that enough Christians catch this vision to fulfill the Great Commission. A survey of the rapid expansion in world population growth makes the need for multiplication urgently clear.

Factors Affecting Personal Follow-up

Personal follow-up, as I have defined and expanded it, does not occur in a vacuum and is not entirely free of restraints which inhibit its growth. There are a number of factors which control and regulate the effectiveness of your discipling ministry. Some of these factors are quite obvious and scarcely need mentioning; others are perhaps less obvious and would be important for you to consider and ponder. The following is by no means an exhaustive list of conditions governing effective personal follow-up ministry, but it is comprehensive and should, if nothing else, stimulate your own evaluation of barriers facing your ministry.

Factor 1: Relationship. Any study of factors affecting personal follow-up ministry must begin by examining the personal needs of the "discipler." It is important that you be in right relationship with the Lord in your own Christian experience. As will be stressed continually throughout this book, personal follow-up is not only methodology, but also life transference. Thus there can be no substitute for a dynamic relationship with Christ in your own life if you seek to be effective in helping someone else grow. There will inevitably be a loss of effectiveness if you try to bypass this rule. There is a subtle temptation, as you begin to gain insights into methods, to begin to rely on a certain method, or perhaps a sequence of instructions, to achieve an effective personal follow-up ministry. I know from personal experience how this can become a source of real ineffectiveness in personal follow-up. My point in making these comments is not to imply that follow-up training is inappropriate or unnecessary (this book is evidence of my conviction of the necessity of this very thing). I am only attempting to point out at the beginning that any important truth can be taken to an extreme and perverted into an error. Methodology training in follow-up is meant to *supplement,* not substitute for, personal-life communication. Paul clearly focuses on the role of life transference in 1 Thessalonians 2:8: "We loved you so much that we were delighted to share with you not only the gospel of God but our lives as well, because you had become so dear to us." A new Christian's growth can be killed in the bud if you focus on methods at the expense of relationship.

Factor 2: Commitment. Multiplication is the product of both personal follow-up and discipleship training and thus is a time-consuming process. Anything that takes time also takes commitment. Perhaps more than any time in history, the average person today is extremely busy. There are many different needs and problems vying for his attention and involvement. The Christian is not immune to these pressures. In fact, the growing Christian perhaps feels them even more acutely because of the time requirements of church involvement which the non-Christian does not face. With the variety of demands on a Christian (i.e., witnessing, worship services, classes, committees, Bible studies, prayer meetings, etc.), a legitimate question is whether or not the time requirements of personal follow-up are valid in light of projected results.

If an individual begins to do some personal follow-up, he is soon faced with a problem of priorities. There is simply not enough time to do everything. He must soon come to a decision on what his priorities are and establish, in the light of his priorities, what are legitimate activities. I hope the previous discussion of the necessity of multiplication has assisted you in perhaps rethinking priorities. Some necessary questions that need to be asked in your own life are:

"Do I believe in the importance of personal follow-up?"
"Am I willing to spend the time necessary to develop disciples?"
"Am I willing to rethink my present involvements and discontinue those which are no longer a priority?"

Asking questions like these and honestly seeking to answer them will go a long way in causing you to become effective in personal follow-up. Only a committed person is willing to spend the necessary time in follow-up. If you are not totally sold on its importance, as soon as problems and frustrations begin to occur, you will leave to find greener, easier pastures. Commitment plays an important role in the development of effective multiplication.

Factor 3: Concentration. Effective follow-up can never take place if you are attempting to work with too many people at one time. Multiplication depends upon spiritually mature and well-trained disciples. This type of disciple is never mass produced, but rather is the product of in-depth, time-consuming, hard work. To achieve true productiveness, you must work with only a few people at a time. Second Timothy 2:2 makes a point about the type of person on whom you should concentrate: *Faithfulness* is the criterion for concentration in the process of multiplication. It is important that you have faithful, trustworthy individuals who will reproduce themselves in this ministry. If you focus your work on a few people for a period of time and they prove untrustworthy, you will have nothing to show for your work. Chapter 7 elaborates on how to choose faithful disciples.

You will need to be totally committed to the concept of personal follow-up to stand against the pressures you are sure to face. The pressure not to concentrate your energies on a few is going to be great. You will be called selfish and unspiritual, among other things. I remember a pastor who was upset by my insistence on this principle. He told me, "I see that the Bible teaches this idea of concentration, but it is clearly unworkable in the church of today. I have too many responsibilities to concentrate my energies." He was unwilling to adopt the biblical method because it would mean changing his traditional method of ministry. What a tragedy.

It is important that you withstand this pressure. This will be possible only if you have a long-range view of your ministry and are not tyrannized by the urgent needs around you. Early in His ministry, Christ chose a core of men and began to pour His life into them. His purpose was to create the leadership necessary to adequately oversee the growth of the early church. In a real sense, Christ staked His entire future effectiveness on these few men. He did not misread God's will in this matter. Under the empowerment of the Holy Spirit, these disciples multiplied, taking the gospel to Jerusalem, Judea, Samaria, and the world (Acts 1:8).

Perhaps the following diagram will be helpful in illustrating the concentration technique employed by Christ. Starting with Christ at the center, the time spent varies inversely with the distance from the center.

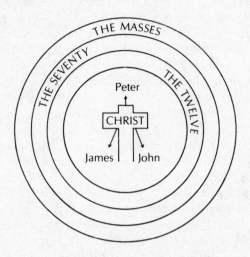

Fig. 2. The Principle of Concentration in the Ministry of Christ

Waylon Moore, in his book *New Testament Follow-up*, discusses various laws governing multiplication. One of the most important is the factor of concentration. He states: "A decision that our ministry will be intensive, rather than extensive will change our whole life. Quality begets quantity. It takes vision to train one man to reach the mass" (p. 68). There is no substitute for the role of personal discipleship development and this can only occur when we concentrate our energies.

Factor 4: Duration. It is going to be exceedingly important to your personal follow-up ministry that you understand and accept certain time requirements. Follow-up is not only a temporary time drain for you, but it will also continue over a period of time, possibly for a year or more. It is important to realize this, not only because you need to be committed to working that long, but also because it will take time for the results of a multiplying ministry to become obvious to those looking on. If you are unsure about the time requirements of multiplication, you will be left without a defense when people criticize you for spending so much time with so few. The truth of this factor is obvious from the discussion of the rate of growth in multiplication over a six-year period (see previous discussion, pp. 120-21). A look at the ministry of Christ is also a convincing demonstration of the truth of this principle.

Christ poured three years of His life into the twelve apostles. Near the end of this time (approximately six months), He spent nearly all of His time with them. Thus Christ, the master Discipler, felt it necessary to do this to insure the massive multiplication of the Christian church over the following quarter of a century. If there had been a better way, Christ would have used it. You would not have been too impressed if you had been an uninvolved bystander at that period of time. There were not more than five hundred followers at the time of Christ's death and many of these were only peripherally involved. Yet Christ was satisfied with His work, for He saw in His disciples the future multiplication of the church.

Waylon Moore stresses this principle and its application to the encouragement of discipleship. He states that it takes multiplication approximately three to five years to become obvious (p. 69). This means it takes that long before people become aware of the growth becoming obvious in their midst. Many laymen and pastors are afflicted with a spiritual shortsightedness. They do not seem to notice the groundwork laid for a ministry program over a period of years, but rather they see only what you are currently doing to achieve growth. This explains why so many have missed the truth of multiplication for so long.

Factor 5: Environment. The final item to be analyzed in our discussion of factors controlling the effectiveness of personal follow-up ministry is the role of environment. This is the spiritual environment the new believer encounters, not his physical environment. The kind of spiritual environment a new believer experiences will play a large part in his subsequent Christian growth, or lack of it. It definitely makes a difference where a new Christian has fellowship. The spiritual temperature of the church in which a new believer finds himself will control to a certain extent the vitality of his life. A lukewarm or cold church environment can be devastating to a new Christian's growth.

A cold or lukewarm environment in a local church strikes at the credibility of what you are teaching the new Christian. In personal follow-up you are talking about the joy of life in Christ, the love of the brethren, the need to witness, the role of Bible study, the fruit of the Spirit, etc. When a person attends a church where these qualities are not evident, he begins to doubt whether you are really being honest with him. A person generally conforms to the characteristics of his environment. A new Christian will conform more readily to carnal Christian living than to spiritual Christian living if that is the prevalent spiritual climate. Perhaps this explains why Christ was so strong in His denunciation of the church at Laodicea in Revelation 3:14-22. Christ says in verses 15 and 16: "I know your deeds, that you are neither cold nor hot. I wish you were either one or the other! So, because you are lukewarm—neither hot nor cold—I am about to spit you out of my mouth." I had always looked at that verse in light of how lukewarmness strikes at the credibility of evangelism, but more recently I have discovered its effect on follow-up as well.

Is your church creating the right spiritual environment for a new Christian's growth? It is important in personal follow-up to insure that he is exposed repeatedly to a vital, vibrant Christian fellowship. If you cannot feel safe in bringing a new Christian to your church, how will you answer him convincingly when he asks you why you are still going there? Environment not only plays a role in a new Christian's growth, but also in the growth of more mature Christians as well.

9

Developing a
Meaningful Relationship

GARY W. KUHNE

The second step in a discipling ministry is to develop a meaningful relationship with the individuals with whom we will be working, whom we will be training, and into whose lives we will be pouring our own. Gary Kuhne gives us some practical pointers on how to do it in this chapter, which is taken from chapter 3 of his book, *The Dynamics of Personal Follow-up.* Following his suggestions will enable us to start moving from the step of follow-up to actual apprenticing, which is the subject of the next section of this book.

9

Developing a
Meaningful Relationship

GARY W. KUHNE

"A friend loves at all times" (Prov. 17:17).

Developing a close friendship with a new believer is a basic ingredient in effectively following up a new Christian, for it involves a nurturing that goes beyond merely the teaching and enforcing of rules. It also involves a loving communication of those rules and a loving communication of a life.

When I first attempted follow-up, I had a difficult time developing relationships with new Christians. The problem was my approach. I was assuming that relationships just naturally occur. In some cases they might, especially if the individual has some areas of interest in common with you. Unfortunately, in personal follow-up you will often be working with someone with whom you have little in common. In this circumstance, it will take concerted effort to build an effective relationship. Over time I discovered a variety of "tools" for building relationships. Along with these came a thrilling sense of spiritual victory in my own life. No longer was I limited to certain types of people for effectiveness in my ministry. I have found a similar joyous response in people I have trained in follow-up ministry. In Christ there is truly neither slave nor free, Jew nor Greek.

Spiritual parenthood has many of the same characteristics as physical parenthood. How many of us could be content merely to be a rule-giver and enforcer with our children? In addition to being an authority figure, a good parent is constantly seeking to know his children better and develop a meaningful relationship with them. This is also true when it comes to effectively following up a new Christian. We do need to be authority figures, i.e., spiritual leaders who communicate the how-to's of growing in Christ. At the same time, however, we must also be developing meaningful relationships with new Christians. The purpose of this chapter is to offer some practical advice on developing this relationship with a new Christian.

Develop an Atmosphere of Loving Concern

One of the first ways to begin developing a meaningful relationship with a new Christian is by being honestly concerned for him, really wanting to be his friend. "A friend loves at all times, and a brother is born for adversity" (Prov. 17:17). Paul clearly teaches this as one of the important elements in his own follow-up ministry. For example, examine the way Paul described his attitude toward the Philippians in Philippians 1:8: "God can testify how I long for all of you with the affection of Christ Jesus." He begins by saying, "God can testify." It is important to understand why he starts this way. Paul doesn't use this term lightly, but rather uses it only when he wants to make something unquestionably clear to us. When he said, "God can testify," Paul knew he was calling an omniscient God to witness to the truth of his statement. This was necessary because of what Paul went on to claim about the way he felt toward them: "God can testify how I long for all of you with the affection of Christ Jesus." What a statement! This describes the point I am trying to make. How much do you really care about the people you are following up? Do you love them with the affection of Christ? If you do, then the relationship is bound to develop; if you don't, the relationship will be hindered. We need to build into our lives the attitude where we can say with Paul, "God is my witness" (RSV), I'm burdened over that new Christian.

I remember working with a young married student. Although I worked hard, I seemed to be getting nowhere in my follow-up. I was unable to gain his confidence and our relationship was a shallow one. One day while thinking about the problem, it occurred to me that I really didn't care about the fellow. I wasn't burdened for his growth, but rather was slightly irritated at the trouble he was causing me. What a sobering and convicting discovery this was! I determined to begin to focus my prayers and concern on him as a person, and to seek to develop the love God desired me to have for him as an individual. It wasn't long before there were some real breakthroughs in follow-up. That young man is now serving God effectively in full-time Christian service.

Do you genuinely want to help the new Christian grow in Christ? Do you honestly care about people? If you feel you need more love and concern to answer in the affirmative, you can pray and specifically ask God to develop that kind of attitude in your life. Through prayer God will give you this type of burden. The Bible doesn't explain why the mechanics of prayer work this way, but there is something about interceding for a person that increases your burden for him.

Pray for specific things. If you run out of things to pray for, start reading the first part of many of Paul's Epistles. There he makes specific prayers for spiritual growth on the part of the new believers. In your prayers insert the name of the person you are following up. If over a period of time you keep praying for him in a disciplined way, God will develop that burden within your heart. You probably won't notice it grow, yet soon you will find yourself sincerely caring for that individual.

There is one exciting implication of this truth I want to emphasize. You can feel a burden for, and thus build a relationship with, someone you would not naturally choose for a friend. When I was in college I had a pastor who helped me a great deal in my own Christian growth and thinking. Once he said something I will never forget: "Before you became a Christian you picked out your friends. After you became a Christian, God began to pick out your friends and often He picks out people you never would." When you are forced into relationships with Christians whom you would never choose to be your friends, it *forces* you to turn to God for the strength and love you need to develop the relationships. In personal follow-up you can't pick and choose who is going to respond to Christ. Sooner or later you are going to find yourself in personal follow-up relationships with people you would not normally choose to spend time with. God can work around that problem. He can give you the attitude you need to develop a friendship with those people.

When seeking to build friendships with new Christians it is important to have an accepting kind of love. Jesus applied this principle of accepting love as He worked with His disciples. His love and concern for those disciples were basic tools in their spiritual growth. They knew He loved them and there was never any doubt in their minds. Even when they failed the atmosphere was one of concerned acceptance. The Lord rebuked them when they failed, but He still loved them and continued to work with them, helping them to learn from their mistakes. In spite of their failures, they knew Christ's love was unconditional.

An important question to ponder is whether you are creating or will create this kind of environment or atmosphere of unconditional acceptance and love for a person. Please don't misunderstand. This doesn't imply overlooking their sinfulness, but rather, it means accepting them in the face of their failings and showing them how to deal with any problems they have. You can love them and help them discover God's way out of it. It is possible to accept the person and at the same time not accept the sinful shortcomings in his life. As you work with people, do you create that kind of accepting atmosphere?

A good way to test yourself is to check out why the new Christian does what you assign him. Is it the result of his motivation to grow in Christ—or is he afraid that if he slips up, you will reject him? Is he performing for your sake, or the Lord's? When pleasing you is the exclusive motivation in a new believer's life, there is something seriously wrong. It's going to be extremely difficult to develop in that person the proper kind of motivation. Are you creating the kind of an atmosphere of love which is helping to motivate the new Christian to grow?

Develop Your Relationship Around Christ

A second major truth in building relationships is to develop your relationship around Christ. It is important to realize that this will take real effort, because the natural thing is to try to develop a relationship around something else. You develop a relationship with one person because he likes basketball, with another because he likes art. Having things in common is a good aid in developing a relationship, but when it becomes the center or focus of your relationship, you become limited in your circle of friends. In 1 John 1:3 John gives us the correct focus for lasting relationships: "We proclaim to you what we have seen and heard so that you also may have fellowship with us. And our fellowship is with the Father and with his Son, Jesus Christ."

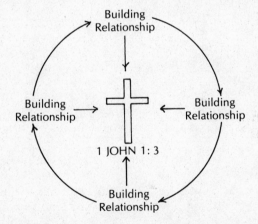

Fig. 3. Focusing Relationships on Christ

John gives Christ as the focal point of true fellowship. He claims that relationships should be developed around knowing

Christ. This does not mean it is wrong to have other things in common with a person you are following up. What it does mean is that often you are going to be put in a follow-up relationship with someone with whom you have little in common. This should not prevent you from having a meaningful relationship and friendship if Christ is at the center.

How do you make Christ the focus? From the very beginning of follow-up with a new Christian, spend the bulk of your time on spiritual things. This doesn't mean lecturing that person, but it does mean devoting most of your time to spiritual communication, creating an atmosphere of spiritual sharing. Make it a natural thing to share with one another what God is doing and what God is teaching you through His Word. This develops naturally only when it is the way you act in the initial stages of that relationship. If you develop your relationship around something else, you will have to force Christ-centered discussion, and it becomes an awkward, unnatural thing. If you develop your relationship from the beginning around Christ and spiritual things, the pattern is set for future openness.

There is another important factor in developing your relationship around Christ. Whenever you are with a new Christian, strive, formally or informally, to share something spiritual. Since formal sharing and teaching occurs naturally when you meet to go over a follow-up appointment, there is no need to elaborate on the formal aspect of this truth. But let me give you a few examples of what I mean by informal sharing:

One tool you might use to develop a relationship with a new Christian is a common interest in baseball. I am talking in terms of youth work here, but the application will be obvious for those working with all age groups. Going to a ball game is a secular activity used for developing relationships. Even in the midst of a game you can be teaching, however. I know one person who has thus shared one of the ways God made a distinct change in his life in the area of attitudes. When he played baseball in school he was aggressively involved in the game. This attitude carried over when he became a spectator. His aggressiveness would express itself beyond yelling and cheering. He also verbally assaulted various referees he didn't think were doing a good job. His attitude was sinful. But God changed him and gave him victory over the problem. By sharing this with the new Christian, he was able to show in a practical way how God makes a difference in the Christian's life. This is a good example of communicating a spiritual truth informally. It may not have been an ideal teaching environment, yet informally he was communicating a deep spiritual truth to that new Christian.

Another example of this informal teaching might involve two women who go shopping together as a tool for developing their relationship. Perhaps there are many people around, and it is hectic. This is a perfect opportunity to share how you used to get frustrated and uptight in this kind of situation, but God has given you patience and peace to keep a good witness for Him in the face of adverse circumstances (Phil. 4:10-13). If God hasn't done that work in you yet, it will be impossible to share in this way and you shouldn't lie about it. However, this example should make the point clear to you that even in secular situations, you can have an informal time of sharing. You ought to be communicating something positive continually.

When I started training my first disciples, I made it a rule never to meet with someone for follow-up or discipleship unless I had something fresh to give him. I wanted to share something new God had taught me or reinforced in my mind during my personal study of the Word. As God has given me strength, I have never since that time failed to communicate a fresh spiritual truth when I met someone for follow-up. You don't have to keep reaching back into your memory. If you are in the Word, the Lord gives you something constructive every time. It might not be a brand-new insight, but it can be a reinforcement of a truth you already knew. And you can always communicate this kind of truth. This is the best way to get the new Christian to the point where he will begin to share with you, too.

A question at this point might be how to motivate people to study the Word. The best way to motivate a new Christian toward Bible study is to use the Bible when you deal with his problems and share how you use it when you are solving your own problems. Jesus motivated His followers to use the Word mainly because He used it. In answer to their questions and problems Jesus quoted the Old Testament 160 times in the presence of His disciples. And that is how you motivate men to use the Word.

Stick-to-it-ness

The next important factor in developing relationships with new believers involves the ingredient of stick-to-it-ness, or patience. It takes time to build relationships. You will not develop a lasting, meaningful relationship with a new Christian in three follow-up appointments. In your first few meetings you can lay the groundwork for a good relationship and set the basic preconditions for it to occur; but the relationship itself will not develop that soon.

The reason for this is obvious. How long does it take you naturally to develop a close relationship with someone? The spiritual realm is no different. The new Christian's relationship with God is going to take time to develop, and it is also going to take time for that new Christian's relationship with you to grow. Friendships will not always grow smoothly, or even at the same rate. Sometimes a new Christian might not seem to be responding at all, yet you need to stick with him.

The fact that a person isn't growing at a certain rate or always being victorious over sin should not discourage you. A person may stumble one week and the next week be renewed from the Word, getting back on the right track once more. Although discouraging, these periods of defeat are not disastrous for one's overall Christian life. This is especially true if one learns from his failures. Learn to have patience in the face of failures. Everyone falls down once in a while and the new Christian you are following up is no exception.

Do not take it personally when the new Christian stumbles.

This is a problem I find often arises among those doing personal follow-up. In other words, you will sometimes be tempted to take the new Christian's stumbling as a reflection on your follow-up expertise. How dare he fail after you did such a good job communicating how not to fail? Of course, sometimes we need to become upset. This motivates us to help our young Christian friend deal with his problems. But when we become upset because our feelings are hurt and our pride is trampled upon, then we are sinning. Our main concern should be that the sin is hurting the new Christian's growth.

Patience is also required to discern the new Christian's attitude in the midst of the failure. Is he repentant, wanting to learn from his mistake, or is he rebellious? It is important that you have discernment at this point. Attitudes at times are not clearly reflected by actions. This is true because actions, in many cases, are controlled by both the past and the present environments in which the person lives. It takes patience and discernment to discover the inner attitude of the new Christian. But you *can* find it because God reveals it to you. It is difficult to detect attitude problems if you don't know what is happening inside an individual. Although you won't totally understand a person's problems and attitudes, you do have the leading of the Spirit to give you a sensitivity others lack.

In his encounter with Ananias and Sapphira in Acts 5, Peter gives us a perfect example of this sensitivity. He was able to see beneath the surface of the problem by detecting wrong attitudes. This example also shows there may be sinful attitudes present even in the right kind of actions. Only in Christ is it possible to gain this type of insight.

Another important element of stick-to-it-ness is being willing to reprove the new Christian when he needs reproof. Whenever he stumbles, it is important that he deal with his problem. In other words, confront him with his sin and then show him how to solve the problem and get back into a right relationship with God. The idea here is to use both the corrective and rebuking aspects of the Word of God as they are revealed in 2 Timothy 3:16-17.

Spend Quality Time Together

"There are friends who pretend to be friends, but there is a friend who sticks closer than a brother" (Prov. 18:24, RSV). The next factor to consider in developing relationships is the role of association. By association I mean spending time with the new Christian. In youth work it is somewhat easier for the association to take place than with adult work, since an adult's time is much more rigidly structured by family responsibilities and similar restrictions. Yet, in spite of the difficulty involved in finding time to spend with an adult who is a new believer, it is still necessary that we do so. For instance, housewives might meet over mid-morning coffee, those in business over lunch. Choose an optimal time for both of you.

When seeking to find activities that aid association, look for something you are already doing to which you could invite the new Christian. This is the key to finding time to do effective personal follow-up. By doing two things at once, you squeeze forty-eight hours into twenty-four. It is possible to piggy-back your time to aid you in association.

One example of how to accomplish this would be to take the new Christian with you when you go to church. The reason you take him with you is not simply to get him to go to church, although that is one reason. It is also for that twenty minutes driving home when you can discuss the sermon. The important thing is just spending time talking together and fellowshiping. Not everything I do for association is feasible for everyone, but we can each find some way to spend time with a new Christian. It might take some effort, but the real problem is one of burden, not time.

Spending time with the new believer is the essence of a truly effective follow-up program. I hope this list of examples will stimulate your own thinking.

1. Going to church
2. Attending church activities
3. Shopping
4. Going to sporting events
5. Washing your car
6. Camping
7. Picnics
8. Holiday activities
9. Short trips
10. Etc.

A new Christian often becomes most open and honest about his victories, defeats, problems, etc., in the informal times. Do all you can to create these all-important times of informal fellowship with a new believer.

Minister to the Total Person

The next factor conditioning the development of effective relationships with new Christians concerns the problem of viewing our role from too limited a perspective. We can sometimes become overly concerned about the spiritual side of a person's life and neglect other aspects involved. Each individual is made up of many parts which form a single whole with all of the parts interrelated. The spiritual affects the social and the social can also affect the spiritual. This interrelatedness is found in every area of a person's life, and because of this you have to deal with more than the spiritual needs of a new Christian.

For example, let's consider the possible relationship between a social problem and a spiritual need in a new believer. An important aspect of personal follow-up is getting the new believer into good Christian fellowship. What will happen if the person you are following up has some social problems that limit his ability to develop good relationships with other Christians? It is obvious that his social problems will cause some spiritual problems as time goes by. It is therefore important that you are able to detect and deal with social problems as one step to seeing real growth in a person's life.

Let's pursue this example further. The new Christian with whom you are working has a problem which is socially restricting. Your purpose in helping him with this problem is not so much to develop a well-polished individual, but rather to help him develop qualities to aid him in having fellowship with other Christians. There are various ways to help someone who is shy. If you have had this problem, show the new Christian what God has revealed to you from His Word to help you deal with it. Just to sit down with him in a follow-up visit and tell him he must get to know people and that God doesn't want him to be shy won't usually solve the problem. It is much more effective to show the new Christian how to do something about his problem and help him actually encounter other people.

Perhaps the person you are following up is blunt, loud, or turns others off. The best thing to do is to sit down with him and tell him his behavior offends other people. Often a person doesn't realize the reaction of others toward his behavior. He has developed a manner of social behavior which he practices, never realizing how it bothers other people. You might also work out some prearranged signal to tell the person when he is becoming offensive, or when he is saying something that should not be said. You do not need to be an expert on social graces to help the new Christian relate to the group.

Perhaps the new Christian needs counseling on family problems. I remember the home situation of one teen-ager I was following up. The father came home drunk every night and beat up the family. Obviously you need to do more than just go over follow-up appointments with such a person. This fellow needed help to face his problems. To really begin to help a new Christian you must get to know more about the circumstances he faces. In this case the new Christian had neglected his devotions. It turned out he wanted to take time for them, but because of the family situation at home he was unable to do so. If I had kept urging him to have devotions without seeking to help this complicating problem, I would only have succeeded in creating frustration and wide communication gaps.

Perhaps the person you are working with has hygiene problems. Who is going to tell him if you don't? You should work toward developing the type of relationship with him where you will be able to give guidance in areas which might prove embarrassing. Your purpose is not to pry, but rather to help him grow in Christ. You are trying to help him become a confident individual. I'm not advocating that you inquire into areas where you are not wanted. Don't force a person to tell you everything. Just be open and receptive. All of this will contribute to developing an attitude of acceptance and mutual confidence, which will greatly aid you in the area of spiritual follow-up. As the new Christian develops confidence in you, he is going to believe more and more of what you say and accept it as authority. This is especially true when it comes to solving problems.

Perhaps the new Christian has a financial difficulty. Maybe his problem is an unworkable budget, since many people just don't know how to make one. Bitter experience taught me how to budget. Perhaps he is going through all kinds of struggle and worry as a result of this problem. To sit down and talk to him about worry will not help him if you can't get to the root of his problem. Again the point here is the need to see each individual as a total person and not just address yourself to one segment of his life.

Remember What He Tells You

Another factor in developing relationships is to remember what the new Christian shares with you. Both as a student and as a full-time Christian worker, I had some bitter experiences in this area. I had a habit of forgetting what people told me. There were times when I met with someone and would forget what his major was in college, or what courses he was taking. This can really become embarrassing. People begin to think you don't really care.

After being embarrassed several times, I developed an easy method of storing information that really helped me with this problem. I began to carry a 3 x 5 card to fill out after I finished meeting with a person. I would jot down all the important information he had told me. Before the next time we met I reviewed the 3 x 5 card. In the initial stages of working with a person it is extremely important to have that information. I mention this problem because it has happened to me and it may well happen to you. If you have a bad memory, start writing things down. People don't usually get turned off by this. It even reassures them that you are concerned enough about them to want to remember what they say.

Be a Leader As Well As a Friend

The next factor in developing a relationship with a new Christian is the need to strike the right balance between being both spiritual leader and friend. In the midst of all this emphasis on friendship and relationship, it is easy to sidestep being a leader. None of us really wants the responsibility of being a leader. We would much rather avoid having to help a new Christian grow in Christ. We prefer to sidestep our responsibility to confront a new believer involved in a sin; we try to put all the responsibility on the Lord to reprove and convict him. This takes the pressure away from us. It is much easier, but much less effective, to remain nonauthoritative in our relationship.

This is one side of the coin. It is also important to realize that it is possible to become too authoritative or problem-oriented. It is best to deal with only one problem at a time, which is quite enough to keep a person busy. Be careful not to make your whole relationship one of constantly telling the new Christian what he is doing wrong. It is much better to have a healthy balance in your relationship of mutual encouragement, sharing of spiritual truths, and counseling. If you keep it balanced you won't create a negative atmosphere of defeat and legalism.

You won't always get positive response from the new Christian as you attempt to be his spiritual leader. There will be negative reactions to deal with as well. You must show him that negative reactions are sinful. If you have been presenting the Word of God to him to point out a particular problem, and he rebels against it, his rebellion is not against you but against God's will. If, however, you have been obnoxious or tried to push too many things on him at one time, then his reaction is your fault. Achieving a good balance is essential.

Another important element in being an effective leader is to deal with problems when they arise and in the order of their priority. There may be more than one obvious problem at a particular time. Deal with the one most crucial to his spiritual growth. If you will deal with problems when they first arise,

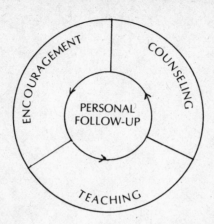

Fig. 4. Keeping Balance in Follow-up

you keep them from becoming major. This honest dealing with problems helps the new Christian develop good habits of Christian living. If, however, you wait too long to deal with a problem, the new Christian will have developed a bad habit. When this happens, it becomes harder to deal with and gain victory over. I am convinced problem-solving is a crucial part of follow-up and discipleship. I hope you will begin to see that it does play an important role and that you are called to be a spiritual leader who gives direction to people in solving their problems. Ask God to help you be an effective friend and leader to the new Christian He has entrusted into your care.

10

Character Development

WILLIAM A. SHELL and LEROY EIMS

The third step in the discipling ministry is to start the process of apprenticing—in-depth training of a followed-up believer in Christian character (discipleship) and how that character can be reproduced in others (disciple making). William A. Shell and LeRoy Eims have collaborated on this chapter, part of which is based on Eims's chapters 7 and 8 in *The Lost Art of Disciple Making,* and the other part on Shell's own ministry, teaching, and training.

The crucial ingredient of discipleship is continual growth in Christian character. The qualities discussed in this chapter must become more and more a part of that disciple's life. These qualities do not magically become ours at the snap of the fingers; they have to be worked on and built little by little into our lives or into the lives of the individuals into whom we are pouring ours.

Shell, a graduate of Baylor University, Westminster Theological Seminary, and Wheaton College Graduate School, came in contact with The Navigators during his Navy enlistment in 1954. Since then he has developed a burden for seeing this ministry being carried on successfully in the local church, and his association with Billie Hanks since 1978 has enabled him to help sponsor Christian Discipleship Seminars in his own denomination through the Evangelism Committee on which he serves. Pastors and churches have been greatly strengthened, evangelistic outreach has increased, and disciples are being trained in larger numbers. And the process begins with character development.

10

Character Development

WILLIAM A. SHELL and LEROY EIMS

"Whatever you have learned or received or heard from me, or seen in me—put into practice" (Phil. 4:9).

Christian character, biblically defined, is a most necessary trait that a believer in Jesus Christ is expected to possess. Not only is the Christian to be different and distinct from the average unbeliever, but he is also to stand head and shoulders above anyone who is known as a person of character. The follower of Christ must be that different from anyone else in the world.

By definition character is "an attribute, quality or property; moral vigor or firmness" (Webster). It is "the aggregate of features and traits that form the apparent individual nature of a person" (Random House). The dictionary then goes on to list a number of individual qualities, including moral excellence, honesty, courage, integrity, and a good reputation. The Bible uses the term only once in the New Testament, where Jesus is identified as "the character of the nature of God." Jesus "is the exact representation of his [God's] being" (Heb. 1:3). The idea here, of course, is that when people saw Jesus, they saw God.

In the same way, when people see Christians they ought to see Jesus Christ in them. So when we speak of Christian character, we are saying that when we see each other and when others see us, the person of Christ should be obvious and visible in us. What we *are*, therefore, is more important than what we *do*. Christian character has to do with what we are as believers in Christ, and it can be developed in our lives.

Furthermore, when we work with our Timothies (see chapter 7), we must help them develop Christian character in their lives. Therefore, in our ministries of disciple making on a personal one-on-one basis, we must focus on building conviction, perspective, excellence, and depth of character in our Timothies, and we do so through our own personal examples and careful training.

Conviction

In the initial stages of follow-up, your Timothy has developed your convictions. He has learned why you memorize the Word, study the Bible, and pray, but this will not sustain him over the long haul. He needs to develop convictions of his own.

Convictions are built in two ways: his own study of the Scriptures, and answering "why" questions. A friend of mine went overseas as a missionary and began to develop a disciple-making ministry. Soon some of the Christians in the country where he was serving came to him with a complaint. They felt that some of the things he was emphasizing were "American ideas." They were not convinced they were for their culture. They thought he was trying to impose purely American concepts on them and they resented it.

Wisely my friend pulled back and suggested they study the Scriptures for themselves to see if the ideas were biblical or American. So they all got their Bibles and went to work. They studied many subjects, such as servanthood, the Word, faithfulness, giving, commitment, discipleship. They looked up and carefully examined scores of passages that bore directly and indirectly on each of these subjects.

It took months, but it was well worth the time invested. I have visited this country on a number of occasions and have never met a more disciplined, committed, and convinced band of men and women. They came to their convictions through a study of the Scriptures, and now the ministry has spread and multiplied. At last report, the major problem they faced was finding a facility large enough to hold their rallies.

On another occasion I was working with a group of people who were having a difficult time seeing the importance of the Word of God in their daily lives. I suggested we do a study on Psalm 119. Nothing deep or exhaustive, just reading through the psalm and noting the various verbs that were used in it. Later we read through the psalm again to find the different words that were used in reference to the Word of God. The third time through we tried to catch the psalmist's attitude toward God's Word. It took quite a while, but they came out of the study with some convictions about its importance from God Himself.

The second way of developing convictions is to have the person jot down all the reasons *why* he should be doing these things. Why have a quiet time? Why pray? Why study the Bible? This can be a real eye-opener. Once he has thought through these things, he no longer sails along on what you have told him. He now has a set of convictions of his own. Convictions are deeper than just personal beliefs. He holds his beliefs, but his convictions hold him.

Perspective

The second thing you must focus on in training is perspective. When a person comes to Christ, he still remains pretty much a self-centered individual. As he begins growing in the Lord, he gets his sights raised a bit. He begins to be aware of the needs of others in the Sunday school class or in the church fellowship. Then a missionary comes to his church and he is made aware of some different needs; he begins to see the world from a different perspective.

His vision is enlarged. His concerns begin reaching beyond himself. He lives his life on a different plane. He is developing a new perspective. This does not come easily. But now he should be to the point in his life where self is fading into the background and the focal point of his vision is the Lord Himself, the will of God, the work of God, and the needs of others.

Excellence

A third thing you should develop in your trainee is a spirit of excellence. He must become proficient in his ministry to others and do it well. His witness, his service, his involvement should reflect the testimony of Jesus Himself, who "has done everything well" (Mark 7:37).

At the International Congress on World Evangelization in Lausanne, Switzerland, in 1974 I met the director of the Toronto Institute of Linguistics. A couple of friends of mine had gone to this excellent school in preparation for service as missionaries. I asked him how they were doing.

He freely admitted that they were not the highest in their class academically, "But," he said, "they are going to come out at the top because they will not permit themselves to settle for less than the best they can do.

"And," he continued, "the motivation seems to come from Jesus Christ Himself."

My friends were committed to excellence. One writer of Scripture prayed:

> May the God of peace, who through the blood of the eternal covenant brought back from the dead our Lord Jesus, that great Shepherd of the sheep, equip you with everything good for doing his will, and may he work in us what is pleasing to him, through Jesus Christ, to whom be glory for ever and ever. Amen (Heb. 13:20-21).

If we are to be equipped with everything good to do God's will, it must be through Jesus Christ. After all, He is the only one who has ever done all things well. So if you would develop a spirit of excellence in those whom you are training, you must bring them to the place where they turn themselves over to Jesus and let Him live His life through them.

This may seem to be hard work, and it is. But if we are to help a person become an effective worker in the kingdom of God, he must have the whats and whys of discipleship firmly in his mind and heart. And he must be skillful in the ministry of helping others build them into their lives. Superficial, slipshod training and learning will not produce the quality of worker who performs with the standard of excellence reflected in the earthly ministry of Jesus Christ.

Depth of Character

The next focus is a continued emphasis on depth in the trainee's walk with God and a deepening of his Christian character. Paul stated, "For the kingdom of God consists of and is based on not talk but power—moral power and excellence of soul" (1 Cor. 4:20, AMPLIFIED).

This is a lifelong emphasis. Such qualities as faith, purity of life, honesty, and humility are never mastered in this life. We continue to grow and mature. This is why John said, "How great is the love the Father has lavished on us, that we should be called children of God! And that is what we are! The reason the world does not know us is that it did not know him. Dear friends, now we are children of God, and what we will be has not yet been made known. But we know that when he appears, we shall be like him, for we shall see him as he is. Everyone who has this hope in him purifies himself, just as he is pure" (1 John 3:1-3).

What are some of these qualities of Christian character that must be deepened in our lives and in the lives of our trainees? A selected, not exhaustive, list and discussion follows.

Health. A character quality not often recognized or acknowledged deals with physical fitness and general health. Lead your Timothy to consider his physical body as the temple of the Holy Spirit (1 Cor. 6:19) and to check to see what activities or habits he needs to commit to Christ to improve his physical health. This includes physical fitness, for which a regular daily exercise program might be necessary. On the other hand, in terms of general health, it might mean committing himself to a specific diet plan or stopping a bad habit, such as smoking, which might be detrimental to the physical body.

Outward witness. What we look like and what we say also reflect what we are. Christlikeness in our personal appearance and in our use of our tongues must also be developed in us and in our trainees. So lead your Timothy to consider his appearance and what he says as part of his Christian witness. Paul said, "I have become all things to all men so that by all possible means I might save some" (1 Cor. 9:22).

In working on the matter of personal appearance, you might need to include such things as stopping biting fingernails and avoiding immodest dress as commitments to excellence. You and your Timothy should consider together various ways in which the tongue can hurt your Christian testimony, through such things as exaggeration, lying, boasting, gossip, slander, and cursing. Then make specific plans to commit the needy area to Christ and start working on it practically.

Purity of life. In a hedonistic age such as ours, Christians must constantly guard themselves in regard to purity in thought, word, and deed. The temptations to compromise, particularly in the Western world, are great, and corruption and impurity are in abundantly visible form around us— newspapers, magazines, movies, radio, and TV. Then there is the subtle temptation to impurity that says, "Well, other Christians are doing it [reading questionable magazines, going to R-rated movies, getting involved with other men or women not their spouses], so why shouldn't I?"

Paul speaks clearly about this: "No temptation has seized you except what is common to man. And God is faithful; he will not let you be tempted beyond what you can bear. But when you are tempted, he will also provide a way out so that you can stand up under it" (1 Cor. 10:13). He also said, "Therefore come out from among them and be separate, says the Lord. Touch no unclean thing, and I will receive you" (2 Cor. 6:17). In the Old Testament God enabled Joseph to resist temptation and he fled from the advances of Potiphar's wife (Gen. 39:11-13).

So guard yourself and help your Timothy cope with the temptations to impurity. Be practical in the help you give. If he continues to yield to immoral thoughts, find out what sort of literature or movies he is exposing himself to; show him some good verses to memorize concerning his point of weakness; and check whether he is "fleeing" from situations which might aggravate his temptations.

The battle for purity is going to be tough, but it is one of the most worthwhile battles we can win through the power of God. This is a victory that strengthens us spiritually and deepens our Christian character.

Servanthood. Another character quality that needs deepening is that of being a servant to others. All too often we want to rule or have positions of prominence rather than unselfishly and unstintingly serving others with no thought of reward or recompense in mind. Jesus had to deal with this issue on a number of occasions. Once He said, "You know that those who are regarded as rulers of the Gentiles lord it over them, and their high officials exercise authority over them. Not so with you. Instead, whoever wants to become great among you must be your servant, and whoever wants to be first must be slave of all. For even the Son of Man did not come to be served, but to serve, and to give his life as a ransom for many" (Mark 10:42-45).

And on another occasion—one the early disciples never forgot—Jesus showed what being a servant means by washing their feet in the Upper Room. When He had finished this unforgettable demonstration, Jesus said, "Now that I, your Lord and Teacher, have washed your feet, you also should wash one another's feet. I have set you an example that you should do as I have done for you" (John 13:14-15). The apostle Paul followed that example in his life and ministry. His commitment to this character quality may be seen in this statement: "For we do not preach ourselves, but Jesus Christ as Lord, and ourselves as your servants for Jesus' sake" (2 Cor. 4:5).

True servanthood is a quality sadly missing in much of twentieth-century Christianity. Yet it is a vital necessity to believers, for when practiced, it reflects to others the reality of the life of Jesus being lived in their lives. According to Paul, a servant puts other people's interests first, yields his rights to others, and is willing to pay the price of being a servant (Phil. 2:3-4). This willingness to be a servant is based on having the same attitude that Jesus had (2:5), which was one of servanthood (2:6-8).

Practically, you can work on yourself and help your trainee develop this character quality by being willing to do menial tasks (see Paul's example in Acts 28:1-3), being available to others when they need you, being observant of the needs of others, and doing more than you are asked (or paid) to do. Furthermore, through practicing servanthood, the quality of humility is deepened in our lives.

Giving. Because Jesus Christ gave Himself for us, we are to give ourselves to Him. Yet we are to give not only of ourselves, but of our resources as well. God wants all aspects of our lives to bring Him glory, including the use of the finances entrusted to us. Solomon said, "Honor the Lord with your wealth, with the firstfruits of all your crops; then your barns will be filled to overflowing, and your vats will brim over with new wine" (Prov. 3:9-10).

Blessing accompanies giving. God Himself said through His prophet, "Bring the whole tithe into the storehouse, that there may be food in my house. Test me in this . . . and see if I will not throw open the floodgates of heaven and pour out so much blessing that you will not have room enough for it" (Mal. 3:10). Jesus reaffirmed this principle when He said, "Give, and it will be given to you. A good measure, pressed down, shaken together and running over, will be poured into your lap. For with the measure you use, it will be measured to you" (Luke 6:38). The apostle Paul also taught this character quality extensively to the Corinthian church (see 2 Cor. 8-9).

You must make sure that you are a biblical giver yourself, then lead your trainee in developing his own convictions and practices in giving. Work on the convictions through Bible study, then develop a workable plan; if your trainee does not have a plan, help him establish one. If necessary, go over his personal expenditures and help him evaluate whether or not his use of money is glorifying to God; then you may want to help him establish a personal budget, which includes regular giving to the Lord.

These and other character qualities mentioned in the Scriptures (see the lists in Galatians 5:22-23, Philippians 4:8, and 2 Peter 1:3-11) do not become ours automatically, but they must be carefully developed and deepened through study of the Word of God, prayer, and hard work. At the same time we can be confident that God will enable us to build these qualities in our lives, for we can depend on Paul's testimony, "Being confident of this, that he who began a good work in you will carry it on to completion until the day of Jesus Christ" (Phil. 1:6).

Transmission by Example

One of the ways in which you can help build these qualities in the life of your trainee is through personal example. Paul was an example to the Thessalonians. "Our gospel came to you not simply with words, but also with power, with the Holy Spirit and with deep conviction. You know how we lived among you for your sake" (1 Thess. 1:5). He also wrote to Philemon, "I pray that you may be active in sharing your faith, so that you will have a full understanding of every good thing we have in Christ" (Philem. 6).

Think of what the apostles must have learned about their own racial prejudices when they observed Jesus with the woman of Samaria (John 4). Think of what they must have learned about concern for the needy as they saw Jesus minister to the sinners, the blind, and the lepers. Think of what they must have learned about dedication and faithfulness as they saw Jesus "resolutely set out for Jerusalem" (Luke 9:51) to go to the cross to die for the sins of men.

Jesus' message was personalized in the everyday affairs of life. His classrooms were the events of the day. He was what He taught. He transmitted His message by His life. For your life to transmit effectively, two things are required: availability and transparency.

Availability. Availability is a two-way street. You cannot train people who are not available, and by the same token, you cannot carry on a meaningful training program if you limit yourself to the formality of the classroom. Jesus and His men were immersed in life together.

John, in reflecting on that incredible experience, spoke of Jesus as the one whom the apostles had looked at and their hands had touched (see 1 John 1:1). You cannot allow yourself to fall into the cuckoo-clock routine where, at the appointed hour, you pop out of hiding and speak your piece and then disappear back into seclusion till it is time for another appearance.

If your objective is to impart to your trainee some intellectual, theological, or philosophical idea for his consideration, it might work. But if you are out to communicate clearly the insights God has given you on discipleship and making disciples so that he might become a spiritually qualified worker, then it will not work. You must be available to your Timothy constantly. You must be deep in your own fellowship with Jesus Christ so that your life might be a focal point for the energizing power of the Holy Spirit to use as a means of being an example to him.

Transparency. The second quality for effective transmission by example is transparency. Cecil and Thelma Davidson are two of the most effective makers of disciples I have ever met. Their lives are open books. Their home has an open door. Their dinner table has been a meeting place for hundreds of men and women through the years. These men and women who today are carrying on their own discipling ministry around the world consider themselves part of the Davidson family.

We should exercise great caution in being transparent with others. It may be dangerous to take off our masks, demolish the barriers, and tear down the walls. People then see us as we are, and often some are disappointed. They expected us to be some combination of St. Theresa and John Calvin, but there we stand, ordinary sinners saved by grace. Still, disciples can learn from our mistakes and failures as well as from our successes.

Too much transparency too soon in the development of a Timothy may cause harm. Jesus knew that and so told His disciples, "I have much more to say to you, more than you can now bear" (John 16:12). On another occasion earlier in His ministry it was recorded of Him, "With many similar parables Jesus spoke the Word to them, as much as they could understand" (Mark 4:33).

So open your life to those who can handle what they see. Share your heart with that inner core as Jesus did. Often the seventy and even the Twelve were not exposed to certain events in the life of Jesus. "After six days Jesus took with him Peter, James, and John the brother of James, and led them up a high mountain by themselves. There he was transfigured before them. His face shown like the sun, and his clothes became as white as the light" (Matt. 17:1-2).

He shared His heart with the same three at Gethsemane. "Then Jesus went with his disciples to a place called Gethsemane, and he said to them, 'Sit here while I go over there and pray.' He took Peter and the two sons of Zebedee along with him, and he began to be sorrowful and troubled. Then he said to them, 'My soul is overwhelmed with sorrow to the point of death. Stay here and keep watch with me'" (Matt. 26:36-38).

Nevertheless, the fact remains that no one can really know you unless you open yourself to him. So we need balance in being transparent with others. I saw this demonstrated at a missionary convention sponsored by Inter-Varsity Christian Fellowship at Urbana, Illinois. A missionary spoke to us and freely admitted his inability to accomplish some of the goals he had set for himself years earlier. He openly confessed his lack of answers for some of the major problems facing his field in the nation where he served. He spoke candidly of his failures as well as his successes.

He contrasted vividly with another man on the program who seemed to be standing on a high ivory pedestal, talking down to us from the vantage point of perfection. The first man seemed to be down there with us, slogging along the same difficult path in which many of us found ourselves, and we identified with him.

At first, being transparent may take the form of sharing with your trainee some of the things you have experienced in your fellowship with the Lord. It may involve your sharing with him some of the victories and defeats, successes and struggles involved in Scripture memory. As you become more involved in his life and he in yours, you will be able to share deeper things, such as the temptations you face, how you handle them, and your battles with the world, the flesh, and the devil.

It is difficult, if not impossible, to help your Timothy effectively unless you are transparent with him. Spiritually qualified workers emerge from the life and ministry of a transparent trainer. Dawson Trotman used to share with us a poem by Edgar Guest that bears on this:

> I'd rather see a sermon
> Than hear one any day.
> I'd rather one would walk with me
> Than merely tell the way.

Training on a One-to-one Basis

The second prime means of building these character qualities in people and equipping teams of trained workers in the church is to give each person individual and personal attention. It means meeting with each one on a man-to-man basis and having clearly in mind what your training objectives are for *that* person. A ministry of multiplication does not come from an attempt to mass-produce disciples on a group level. There must be individual, personal time with each person with whom you are working and whom you are training. If you want others to disciple individually, you must work with your potential workers in the same way.

This brings us to some important questions. What do you do in these one-on-one sessions? How often should you have them? Where should you meet?

Where? Anywhere that is convenient. A friend of mine

meets the man with whom he is working for lunch in his car in the parking lot near where the man works. Each takes a sack lunch and they meet once a week. What do they do? They share with one another what God has been showing them in their quiet times. They spend some time in the Word together. They usually check each other out on their newly memorized Scriptures. They discuss the ministry God has given them. The man is usually full of questions regarding the ministry of discipleship in the lives of people with whom he is working. Then they pray together.

No hard and fast rule dictates how their time is spent. Occasionally they will spend most of their time praying. On other occasions, the man will bring along a friend from the office to whom he has been witnessing. The three of them meet at a restaurant and the trainer helps his friend in evangelism. He gives his testimony and shares the gospel with the non-Christian. So they accomplish two things: they present the gospel, and the trainee learns something in the process.

A commitment to working with individuals will mean a single-minded approach to life and the ability to sidestep many opportunities that might present themselves. You *could* do many things, but there is one thing you must do if you are to be used of God to fulfill this ministry: you must *concentrate* on the personal needs of each person whom you train.

Once you have determined this to be your course, you will have to learn how to say "no" graciously. If God has given you the vision for a ministry in depth, it does not necessarily mean that you will have no ministry in breadth. In fact, if your potential workers become men and women who can effectively lead and meet the needs of others, your minsitry will multiply much faster than you could do it yourself. So perseverance and patience are cardinal virtues in the life of the trainer.

Does this mean that you cannot have a public ministry? That someone else will preach all your sermons? Or teach your Sunday school lessons? That you will have to turn down all invitations to speak at special meetings and conferences? Of course not. Did Jesus have a public ministry? Yes, and quite a broad one at that. He preached in houses, synagogues, on the hillside, at the seaside (Mark 2:1; 3:1; 4:1; Matt. 5:1). He included His example of preaching in the training of the Twelve. He said, "Let's go somewhere else—to the nearby villages—so I can preach there also. That is why I have come" (Mark 1:38).

You must discipline yourself to think in terms of training, to look on the various facets of your ministry as opportunities to build in depth into the lives of your trainees. This will enable you to keep your priorities straight, and you will be able to gauge what you do by how it contributes to your prime objective of developing spiritually qualified workers. Your ministry will have meaning only as it contributes to the maturing of these men.

What was the ministry of the apostle Paul? Evangelist, theologian, missionary strategist, church planter, teacher, and apostle. But always there were a few key men around him. On one occasion, "he was accompanied by Sopater son of Pyrrhus from Berea, Aristarchus and Secundus from Thessalonica, Gaius from Derbe, Timothy also, and from the province of Asia Tychicus and Trophimus" (Acts 20:4). He used his broad ministry to concentrate on a few.

In writing to the Corinthians, Paul reminded them that he was their spiritual father and challenged them to imitate him. He then informed them that he was sending Timothy to minister to them (see 1 Cor. 4:15-17). Now the question is, If Paul wanted them to imitate *him*, what good would it do to send Timothy? As we read Paul's explanation for sending Timothy, we discover a startling truth. When Timothy came to Corinth, it would be exactly the same as though Paul had come to them. Timothy was more than just an "instructor"; He was actually an extension of the life and ministry of Paul.

Paul could do that because he had confidence in the men he had trained. He later told the Philippians, "I hope in the Lord Jesus to send Timothy to you soon, that I also may be cheered when I receive news about you. I have no one else like him, who takes a genuine interest in your welfare. For everyone looks out for his own interests, not those of Jesus Christ. But you know that Timothy has proved himself, because as a son with his father he has served with me in the work of the gospel. I hope, therefore, to send him as soon as I see how things go with me" (Phil. 2:19-23).

Likeminded, trustworthy, competent men are not made on a production line like automobiles in an assembly plant. They are carefully and prayerfully developed under the loving guidance of a wise trainer who spends much time on his knees praying for them. In an age of nearly instant everything, we must discipline ourselves to think in terms of quality.

It takes time. It takes effort. It means times of joy and times of tears. It means your life, but it also means success in carrying out the Great Commission.

11

Discipleship as a Lifestyle

GENE WARR

One of the most experienced and dedicated disciple makers we will find anywhere in the world today is Gene Warr, a layman and businessman in Oklahoma City. He is the president of the Warr Company, a real-estate investment corporation, and the author of a practical Bible study for men. This chapter is taken from his book *You Can Make Disciples* (Word, 1978), which is essential to the library of every disciple maker.

Lorne Sanny, president of The Navigators, wrote these significant words in the foreword: "Gene Warr is a disciple maker. He is also a stimulator. He has been doing it for years and getting others to do it. Therefore, the material presented in this book has been tested in real-life experience. It is a veritable handbook of how-to's for those who are willing to obey Jesus' command to go and make disciples." It couldn't be stated better than that.

The chapter selected for this book deals with some necessary negatives, warnings of the cost of ministry and certain misconceptions some people have about the disciple-making approach. But Warr's inimitable style will make us willing to pay the cost and help us overcome any misconceptions we might have had.

11

Discipleship as a Lifestyle

GENE WARR

"And the things that thou hast heard of me among many witnesses, the same commit thou to faithful men, who shall be able to teach others also" (2 Tim. 2:2, KJV).

Multiplication works. In the previous chapters of *Discipleship* we have seen it in its biblical context and in its practical application in today's church. It is God's time-tested plan for ministry. Disciples have been made over the centuries, and now there are representatives of Christianity in every nation on earth. Moses poured his life into Joshua; Elijah poured his life into Elisha; and on and on. Jesus to the Twelve; the Twelve to others; Paul to Timothy; Timothy to faithful men; those faithful men to others also.

Why I Am Committed to a Multiplication Ministry

I am committed to a multiplication ministry for three reasons: the brevity of life, a sense of stewardship, and a desire for my life to count for God.

First, *the brevity of life.* The Bible teaches that life is like a vapor. Swifter than a weaver's shuttle, it is like a tale that is told. It is fleeting like water poured out upon the ground which cannot be gathered up again. I can identify with David when he cried out, "Cast me not off in the time of old age; forsake me not when my strength faileth" (Ps. 71:9, KJV). I understand that. And when David prayed, "Now also when I am old and greyheaded, O God, forsake me not; until I have

167

shewed thy strength unto this generation, and thy power to every one that is to come" (Ps. 71:18, KJV).

The only way I can show the power of God to "everyone who is to come" is by investing in the lives of people who will invest in the lives of other people who will invest . . . and that way, by the grace of God, I can show the power of God to generations yet to come.

There are even some promises regarding this: Isaiah wrote, "Even to old age I am the same and to (the time of) gray hair I will bear you. I have made you and I will carry you: even I will bear you and save you" (Isa. 46:4, MLB). A psalm promised, "In old age they shall still be bearing fruit. They shall be full of life and vitality" (Ps. 92:14, MLB).

Second, *a sense of stewardship.* We refer to life as "my life." It is precious. In Job 2:4 Satan says, "All that a man hath will he give for his life." But why do we call it *"my* life"? I have a responsibility for the life that God has given me. I didn't manufacture it. I don't sustain it. It is something which God has loaned me for a short time while here on earth, and I believe I have a responsibility to invest it where it will count most. The psalmist says, "Let everyone bless God and sing his praises, for he holds our lives in his hands. And he holds our feet to the path" (Ps. 66:8-9, LB).

Third, *I want my life to count for something worthwhile.* I'd hate to reach the end of the road and have it said of me as it was said of an old couple in Somerset Maugham's *Of Human Bondage:* "It was as if they had never lived at all." I don't want that to happen to me. I want to *live* and pass on abundant life in Christ to many, many others. I can do it through a ministry of spiritual multiplication, reproducing myself many times over in a disciple-making ministry. And so can you.

Disciple Making Is a Costly Ministry

To be used of God to make disciples, we must be willing to pay the price . . . and it is a costly ministry.

Costly in Quantity of Time. We must be constantly on call. It takes time to drive to a restaurant to eat a meal with the person we are training, it takes time to go on a trip with that trainee, and it takes time to do other things that will make a reproducing disciple of him. Moses prayed, "So teach us to number our days, that we may apply our hearts unto wisdom" (Ps. 90:12, KJV). Our time will not be our own. We must be available to those whom God has called us to help.

Costly in Lack of Recognition. Paul said, "Yet we urge you to have more and more of this love, and to make it your ambition to have no ambition! Be busy with your own affairs and do your work yourselves. The result will be a reputation for honesty in the world outside and an honourable independence" (1 Thess. 4:11-12, PHILLIPS). The discipling ministry is not the kind that gets notoriety in the church paper. Neither is there a place to check it on our offering envelopes. Although this is rapidly changing, discipling has traditionally been an unrecognized work in the kingdom of God.

Costly in Inconvenience. We are servants to those we intend to help. Jesus said, "But I am among you as he that serveth" (Luke 22:27, KJV). We must meet the needs of those God has chosen for us to help. And this means leaving the TV set during a Dallas-Los Angeles playoff game, with the score tied and only a few minutes to play, when a call for help has come from the person I am training. We meet these needs on God's terms, not ours. We are servants to the body of Christ.

Costly in Hurt. At times we will be hurt by those whom we are trying to help. On this subject Paul wrote, "And I will very gladly spend and be spent for you; though the more abundantly I love you, the less I be loved" (2 Cor. 12:15, KJV). In the same letter he added, "I pray that you will live good lives, not because that will be a feather in our caps, proving that what we teach is right; no, for we want you to do right even if we ourselves are despised" (2 Cor. 13:7, LB). Paul was willing to suffer the cost of being despised if the hurt would help the Corinthians. He went on, "We are glad to be weak and despised if you are really strong. Our greatest wish and prayer is that you will become mature Christians" (2 Cor. 13:9, LB). Some in whom you have invested your life will turn their backs on you and walk away. Others may even become bitter toward you. Still others will go so far in the school of discipleship and no further. All of these will hurt. We must not become discouraged in our calling, for some of those who fall by the wayside will eventually come back and want to get back on the path. Others are certainly better off for the help they have received than if they had received none at all.

Costly in Vulnerability to Exposure. Paul wrote to Timothy: "But thou hast fully known my doctrine, manner of life, purpose, faith, longsuffering, charity, patience, persecutions, afflictions, which came unto me at Antioch, at Iconium, at Lystra; what persecutions I endured: but out of them all the Lord delivered me" (2 Tim. 3:10-11). In the Phillips translation, this same verse reads: "But you, Timothy, have known intimately both what I have taught and how I have lived. My purpose and my faith are not secrets to you. You saw my endurance and love and patience as I met all those persecutions and difficulties."

You can't hide from the one you are helping! The one you are helping will see your feet of clay. A disciple will know your weaknesses because on an eyeball-to-eyeball basis, there is no place to hide.

Costly in That You Will Be Tunneling While Others Are Climbing. Jeremiah said to Baruch, "And seekest thou great things for thyself? Seek them not" (Jer. 45:5, KJV). You will have to tunnel while others climb. But tunneling is usually not very dangerous. When you climb sometimes rocks are kicked off and hit the people coming behind, but in tunneling usually anyone can safely follow. Discipling people is a tunneling ministry.

Costly in Seeing Your Weaknesses Reproduced. As it is in nature, so it is true in the Spirit . . . we reproduce in kind.

This is why "cross training" is so important. This happens naturally in the church through the numerous relationships made in Sunday school and in the worship services. In cross training the disciple gets spiritual help from others besides yourself, so that all of your weaknesses aren't reproduced in that one. What Samuel learned as a little boy in Eli's family (bad habits of child-rearing), he reproduced in his own children. Then, at the end of Samuel's life the people saw the grave weaknesses in his children and asked that his children not be the rulers over them. A king had to be chosen from elsewhere. We do reproduce in kind.

Costly in Your Life. This is the main price we pay if we are going to disciple people. God said through Isaiah to his people Israel, "Since thou wast precious in my sight, thou hast been honourable, and I have loved thee: therefore will I give men for thee, and people for thy life" (43:4, KJV). That is exactly what it will cost you—your life.

Misconceptions About the Ministry of Disciple Making

Because the ministry of multiplication is so effective, it will be fought tooth and nail by our enemy the devil. He will strive to combat it in every way possible, and one of his best tools is to use misconceptions. We need to be alert to these to fulfill our ministries of disciple making. There are a number of misconceptions that can hinder our work:

That an emphasis on discipleship neglects evangelism. Our ministries are not *either/or,* but *both/and.* We are not only to disciple others, but we are also to win others to Christ. The end result of all one-on-one training develops a lifestyle of spiritual reproduction (see chapter 8, pp. 120-21).

That the congregation at large is neglected when one-on-one discipleship is emphasized. After His resurrection Jesus appeared to Peter and asked him three times if Peter loved Him. When Peter replied in the affirmative, Jesus then told him three times to "feed my lambs," "feed my sheep," and "feed my sheep" (John 21:15-17).

"Feeding sheep" means ministering to the multitude of the family of God. It is not the same thing as one-on-one discipleship. Paul later pointed out that God has given special gifts to some members of the body in order that they, the pastors/teachers, may develop the saints (the Christian community) to go out and do the ministry (Eph. 4:11-12). Jesus Himself carried on both a public and private ministry. Again the answer is both/and, not either/or.

That you have to be a finished product to help others become disciples. You only have to be one step ahead of others to help them down the entire length of the road of life. Even Paul did not claim to be completely mature when he trained Timothy and others.

That clergymen can't do it because they are too busy. Many are already doing it, but they had to reassess their priorities and become willing to pay the price.

That you must be an ordained minister to do it. Sometimes even clergymen and theologians do not know how to reach others face-to-face. W. A. Criswell tells the story of a group of modernistic theologians who met with the Lord Jesus. The Lord asked these famous and illustrious theologians, "Who do men say that I am?" And they replied, "Some say that you are John the Baptist raised from the dead; some say that you are Jeremiah or one of the prophets; and even some say you are the Christ, the Son of God." Then the Lord asked the theologians, "But who do *you* say I am?" And the theologians gave a learned answer, "Thou art the ground of being, thou art the leap of faith into the impenetrable unknown, thou art the existential, unphraseable, unverbalized, unpropositional confrontation with the infinitude of inherent, subjective experience." The Lord turned sadly away.

That it is an unrealistic approach. There is the story of the man who told Dwight L. Moody, the famous evangelist, that he didn't like his method of evangelism. Moody said he wasn't too happy with it himself, then asked the man what method he used. The man answered, "Oh, I don't have any method." Moody replied, "Well, I like mine better than yours."

True, if those who had begun the multiplication process thirty-two years ago had succeeded with every convert and disciple, the entire world would by now have been totally reached for Christ. This is the reason quality is so important. Weak links in the chain do break the reproductive process. Every time you lose a link you cut your ultimate production in half. This is the reason why quality discipling is so important.

That you must see immediate, measurable results. It took Jesus three years to train twelve people . . . and really only three in great depth. Why are *we* in such a hurry? In our society of "instantness" we want instant disciples. There is no such thing in all the history of the church.

That it will always succeed. Obviously, it won't. There will always be weak links. The story of Gehazi, a disciple of Elisha in 2 Kings (5:15-16, 21-27), is a good example of this. Gehazi had every opportunity to learn. He saw Elisha heal the waters of the city which had produced barrenness; he saw bears attack the young men who had made fun of Elisha; he heard Elisha pray and saw God's answer as He filled ditches with water so that the men and animals could drink when fighting the Moabites; he saw the widow supplied supernaturally with enough oil to sell and pay off her debts and have sufficient remaining to live on; he saw the raising of the dead son of the Shunammite woman; he saw the poisoned pot of vegetables, eaten by the sons of the prophets, made pure by Elisha's throwing in a handful of meal; he saw Naaman the leper healed. And yet, in the end, Gehazi failed. One of the great misconceptions in working with people is that you always succeed. You don't.

My own stumbling efforts to make disciples certainly have not always been crowned with success. That's one of the things that breaks my heart. There are many reasons for lack of success.

Compromise for social approval—I remember a young man whom I will call Bill. After some seminary training Bill came to our city deeply disillusioned with Christianity and his own walk and life. As I began to meet, talk, and pray with him, I found that he knew nothing of the basic disciplines of the Christian walk. I shared these with him, and he responded positively to the idea. He began to meet the Lord morning by morning in a quiet time, began to memorize Scripture, was effectively reaching out in witness to others, and was doing an excellent job of in-depth Bible study. He was capable of making a good living with his hands, which he was doing, when one day a small church in Oklahoma City called him to be their pastor. He accepted. The Lord blessed his ministry there, and we continued to fellowship. It wasn't long until a larger church in a distant state gave him a call, and he responded. In the larger situation, he was in a more affluent society. He began to drink socially, then steadily began to seek out the companionship of other women, and consequently lost his wife and family, and ended up a suicide in a motel. My heart yet yearns for him.

Love of money—Then there was another whom I'll call George. George was a sharp fraternity man, socially very acceptable, a good businessman, and was seemingly sitting on top of the world. When he was about thirty years of age the claims of Christ were made clear to him for the first time, and he made that commitment. Then the roof fell in. He lost his job, moved to another city with his family, had difficulty finding employment, but finally, by the grace of God, was able to get a good job. He then began to move up in the economic scale again. He continued to walk with the Lord and encouraged others. But his desire for wealth began to shade his judgment, and he took a job which put him in compromising positions time and time again. Finally, the temptation was too great, and he succumbed. He left his wife and children. The last time I heard, he had married a widow older than himself, and was living on her money. George and I had spent literally hours together studying the Bible, praying together, going out on ministry assignments together. Often on my knees weeping in prayer, I wondered and asked God where I failed him.

Lack of wholeheartedness—Let me tell you about a man whom I'll call Stan. Everyone liked Stan. He had a dear wife. They were active in their church, Sunday school, and home Bible study. For perhaps two years, they were about as faithful a couple as you could see. They grew and grew to a certain point, and then stopped—stagnated.

Today, Stan is relatively ineffective as a husband, as a father, and as a witnessing Christian. There were some issues in his life which he refused to deal with. One was submission to authority. He held on to a streak of rebelliousness. Second, unfaithfulness. Making promises and not keeping them. Starting jobs and not completing them. Third, a refusal to operate with a margin. This was true with time as well as with money. Fourth, a lack of wholeheartedness. Doing things as he wanted to do them or felt like it, instead of an all-out effort doing it as unto the Lord. Fifth, just plain laziness, which in the final analysis is self-centeredness. Today, as I look at Stan, and recognize the infinite potential in his life, it grieves me to see him on the shelf outside the will of God.

Conclusion—Stories of failure are sobering. You ask me why I don't quit. The reason I don't, is because, thank God, there are other stories, too. They center around a question I am often asked, "Is it really worth investing your life in people?" Let me tell you how worthwhile it is.

Paul was newly married and a youth director in his church. But he was fired from a job on which he was depending to support his wife and to see him through school. He was fired, not for doing a poor job as a youth director, but because he couldn't preach—which he had not been hired to do.

I thought the young man should know why he was fired, so I asked him to come down to my office. I told him he got fired because he didn't know how to get along with adults. He had been called to work with young people and had done an excellent job with them, but unless he learned how to get along with adults, he would always be in trouble. I then asked him what he was going to do with his schooling, and at that point he didn't know.

I counseled with Paul for a while, then told him I would help him financially with his schooling, but there would be one requirement on his part. Every time he came to get his monthly check he would have to spend two hours with me. We started on that basis, and I began to invest my life in his.

Besides meeting regularly, I took him on trips with me. I remembered that he had been fired for not being able to preach, so on one trip to Weatherford, Texas, I decided we'd work on that weak point. I asked him, "Paul, what do you know the most about in your Christian life?"

He thought a while, then replied, "I believe maybe the quiet time."

I said, "OK, what do you know about the quiet time?"

He began to tell me, and I said, "Write that down." That day on the way to Weatherford and back we developed a message on the quiet time, which I believe he is still preaching. It had emerged out of his life.

Some months later Paul met a fellow student by the name of Bob and began to invest in his life some of the things I had been sharing with him. Still later Bob became the youth director in my church, so I carried on with him where Paul had left off. Bob led a pair of twins, Rick and Bob, to Christ, then began to invest his life in theirs. One of them is now a pastor, the other a Christian education director. The first Bob also led Lynn to the Lord, trained him individually over a period of time, and he is now about to enter a Christian education ministry on a full-time basis.

These men have in turn led others to Christ and poured their lives into them, and that chain in the ministry goes on reproducing. And it is only one of a series of chains that began even before Charlie Riggs started investing his life in mine. For Charlie had been trained by Dawson Trotman.

Is it really worth investing our lives in people? As far as I am concerned it certainly is. Here are seven generations and still growing:

> Dawson Trotman
> Charlie Riggs
> Me
> Paul
> Bob
> Rick, Bob, and Lynn
> Many others

Multiplication works. Discipleship as a lifestyle can and will reproduce to many generations.

12

The Need
of the Hour

DAWSON E. TROTMAN

No book on discipleship that claims to include the best from the most experienced disciple makers would be complete without an excerpt from the writings of Dawson Trotman. "Daws," as he was known to those who knew him, was a visionary who was not afraid to put his visions into shoe leather and find practical ways of implementing them. Of all men in this century he was most used of God to rediscover the biblical principles of discipleship and disciple making and restore them to the church of Jesus Christ.

Though he was not an active churchman, yet he was the founder and first president of The Navigators, a Christian service organization that built on his vision, and to help the church around the world begin implementing the biblical concept of discipleship training. Others who have been influenced and helped by The Navigators have developed strategies and curriculums that have worked very well in church programs and ministries. But Daws remains the one who put it all together a few decades before others in this century even began thinking about discipleship.

The last chapter of this book is taken from the booklet *The Need of the Hour* (NavPress, 1957, 1975), which was derived from a message that was a burden on Daws's heart in 1956. William Shell heard Daws give this message in Dallas, Texas, in the spring of 1956, a few months before Daws's death.

If you read this message with an open heart and a receptive mind, you will never again be the same. The need of which Daws spoke in the 1950s is still as great in our world today, and the challenge to be true disciples of the Lord Jesus Christ still needs to be clearly sounded. Trotman though dead yet speaks, and we need to listen, respond, obey, and apply. When we do, God will multiply our ministry into unbelievable and fascinating directions.

12

The Need of the Hour

DAWSON E. TROTMAN

"Jesus . . . said, 'All authority in heaven and on earth has been given to me. Therefore go and make disciples'" (Matt. 28:18-19).

What is the need of the hour? That depends upon the person who is thinking about it. If I'm walking along the street and see a beggar with a tin cup, what's the need of the hour? A dime. If a woman is being taken to the hospital, what's the need of the hour? A doctor.

But in Christian work, what is the need of the hour? I started to list the things that we often feel are *the* need—those things which if supplied, would end our troubles.

Some say, "Well, if I just had a larger staff . . ." Would more staff be the answer? Today many a minister would like to have an assistant and many a mission would like to have more missionaries. The cry of returned missionaries is always for more men and women to fill up the ranks—to them, the need of the hour.

Others say, "We don't need more workers, but if we had better facilities . . . if we just had more office space and more buildings and bigger grounds and a base of operation . . . if we had an attractive conference grounds . . . then we could do the job."

In certain areas of the world they say it's communications we lack, or better transportation, or better means to take care of health. The need of the hour on many a mission field is merely a radio. But if you get that radio, then there's another

179

need followed by something else and something else. Many feel it is literature. I hear that in my travels all over the world, "We just lack literature."

I know of people today who are saying, "If we could just get into a certain place." For years people have been on the borders of Nepal saying, "If we could just get in." To them the need of the hour is an open door into Nepal. Right now hundreds of people are saying, "If we could just get into China." The Bible says, "My God shall supply all your needs." If the need were an open door into China, why doesn't God open it? "These things saith He that is holy, He that is true. He that hath the key of David, He that openeth, and no man shutteth; and shutteth, and no man openeth . . . I have set before thee an open door."

Paul found closed doors, but closed doors to him weren't the problem. I believe those closed doors were used of God to show him the open doors he was to go through next. If God wanted to put His hand over the great country of China tonight, He could open the door in forty-eight hours.

Some say, "We need time. If we just had more time." Others say, "If I just weren't so old, if I were young again." People have said to me, "Daws, if I had known when I was twenty years old what I know now, I could have done a hundred times more for the Lord. Why didn't I?"

Often the biggest need of the hour seems to be money. "If we just had money . . . That's the answer to a larger staff, more facilities, literature, communications, and transportation . . . If we just had money."

What is the need of the hour? Frankly, I don't believe it is any of these. I am convinced that the God of the universe is in control and He will supply all of these needs in His own way and in His own time, all else being right.

Let me tell you what I believe the need of the hour is. Maybe I should call it the answer to the need of the hour. *I believe it is an army of soldiers, dedicated to Jesus Christ, who believe not only that He is God, but that He can fulfill every promise He has ever made, and that there isn't anything too hard for Him.* It is the only way we can accomplish the thing that is on His heart—getting the gospel to every creature.

In 1948 I was in Germany for six days. I had been put in touch with Colonel Paul Maddox, Chief of Chaplains for all of Europe, and through his recommendation to the Commanding General I got into Germany. I invited fifty German fellows to meet with me for three days, and twenty-five of them came. I talked to them every evening for three hours, beginning to lay before them the Great Commission and the idea that I felt Germany not only needed to hear the Gospel, but that Germans themselves needed to obey the Great Commission by sending missionaries.

I gave them the opportunity to ask questions during the meetings and every once in a while a hand would go up. I was trying to lay upon their hearts the very thing the Lord laid on the hearts of the disciples when He told them to go to every creature, make disciples of every nation, start in Jerusalem and go to the ends of the earth. One German spoke up, "But, Mr. Trotman, you don't understand. Here in Germany some of us right in this room don't even have an Old Testament; we only have a New Testament." But I pointed out, "When Jesus Christ gave these commandments, they didn't have even a New Testament."

Later one of them said, "But, Mr. Trotman, we have very few good evangelical books in this country. In America you have thus and so." I asked, "How many books did the disciples have?"

A little further on one of them asked, "Is it true that in America you can hear the Gospel any day?" I answered, "Yes." He said, "If we had that . . . but we can't get the message out on any radio." I said, "But the disciples had never heard of a radio."

They said, "You have automobiles, we ride bicycles." I reminded them, "The disciples didn't have bicycles. Jesus rode a borrowed burro."

Now these questions didn't come up one right after the other or they would have caught on, but arose during the nine hours together. Finally one fellow spoke up, "In America you have money. I work twelve hours a day for sixty cents. We don't have much money." I replied, "The disciples were sent out without purse and without script."

Every excuse in the book was brought up. "We don't have this, and we don't have that. We don't have buildings; we don't have facilities." Each time I replied, "But the Twelve didn't and He sent them out."

Then finally near the end one fellow, a little older than the rest and with almost a bitter expression on his face, got up and said, "Mr. Trotman, you in America have never had an occupation force in your land. You don't know what it is to have soldiers of another country roaming your streets. Our souls are not our own." I responded, "The disciples lived at the time Jesus Christ lived and their souls weren't their own. The Roman soldiers were in charge."

Then it dawned on me in a way I had never considered before that when Jesus Christ sent the Eleven out, He let a situation exist which was so bad that there could never be a worse one. No printing presses, no automobiles, no radios, no television, no telephones, no buildings, not one single church, no uniforms, nothing for the vestry . . . He didn't even leave them a little emblem.

He left them only a job to do, but with it He said, "All power is given unto Me in heaven and in earth. Go ye therefore. . . ." (KJV). What does the "therefore" mean? It means, "I have the power to give you the order and I have the power to back you to the hilt." He was all power in heaven and earth . . . not just heaven, but in the earth; all power, not part of the power, but all power, which means power over the Romans and power over the Communists.

Earlier Jesus Christ had said to this same little group, "Verily, verily, I say unto you, he that believeth on Me. . . ." He that what? ". . . believeth on Me, the works that I do shall he do also; and greater works than these shall he do." Do you believe this is true? Or must you say that for a moment it makes you stop to wonder. Could it possibly be true that the

Son of God would say to a human being, "The things that I do, you shall do, and greater things than these you shall do"?

I believe with all my heart that the reason so many wonderful Christians don't accomplish more in their lives is they don't believe Jesus meant what He said. They have never come to the place where they believe that the all-powerful One who commissioned them could enable them to do these greater works. The last thing He said was, "All power is given unto Me. I'm giving you your orders now. Go and teach all nations and see that every created being hears the Word."

Now we think it is going to be a tough job, even with the printing press, the radio, the airplane, and modern medicine. What do you think the early disciples thought about it? When Paul wrote to the Romans he said, "I thank my God that your faith is spoken of throughout the whole world" (1:8, KJV). When he wrote to the Thessalonian church he said, "For our gospel came not unto you in word only, but also in power, and in the Holy Ghost, and in much assurance" (1 Thess. 1:5, KJV). And he said to the Thessalonians, who were not even as strong as the Bereans, "For from you sounded out the Word of the Lord not only in Macedonia and Achaia, but also in every place your faith to God-ward is spread abroad" (1 Thess. 1:8, KJV).

How did the message go? Not by telephone, not by television, but by tell-a-person. That's the only method they had. It was as simple as that. Everyone was to tell someone else. "I cannot help but speak the things which I have seen and heard" was the impelling force. That's how it spread, and it did spread. They didn't need the printing press and they didn't need materials.

Over in England they really went for Bible study and memory materials. It was hard to get them to see their value at first, but when they did, some of them felt they were a necessity. One rainy night during the Billy Graham crusade at Wembley Stadium, around three thousand came forward at the invitation. Two clergymen came running up to me, "Mr. Trotman. Mr. Trotman, we ran out of materials! What will we do?" I said, "Relax. They probably ran out of them at Pentecost, too!" They looked at me for a minute and, obviously getting the point, said, "That's right!"

The answer is the man, not materials. Maybe the greatest problem today is that we try to put into printed form that which should go from lip to ear and heart to heart. We deemphasize materials and people can't understand why. Materials are tools. Tools by themselves are useless. If there were a young fellow beginning his study of medicine who had all the necessary instruments for a major operation, and an old doctor who just had a razor blade and a plain, ordinary crooked needle and some store string, I'd put myself into the hands of the old doctor for surgery rather than this boy over here with all his instruments, wouldn't you? It's not only the tools; it's the man who has the tools in his hands.

What is the need of the hour? I'll tell you the need of the hour. It is to believe that our God controls the universe, and when He said, "The earth shall be filled with the knowledge of the glory of the Lord, as the waters cover the sea," He meant it. That is exactly what is going to happen. The earth will be filled with the knowledge of the glory of the Lord!

Today more people than ever in a lot of our civilized countries know about Jesus Christ because of the radio, literature, mission societies, Billy Graham, etc. But they only know about Him; they don't know Him. The Book says, "The earth shall be filled with the knowledge of the glory of the Lord, as the waters cover the sea." How much does the water cover the sea? Do you think that every square inch of sea has water in it? Yes! You have no illustration more complete, "as the waters cover the sea." That's how every tongue and tribe and nation in every single nook and corner of this earth is going to hear about Jesus Christ and His glory.

What is the need of the hour? It is to believe that "Thy God reigneth." The rain isn't coming down like you feel it should in order to have good crops. Can He send it if it's necessary? If He doesn't, can you say, "Thank you, Lord"? That's what He wants. "In everything give thanks."

You don't need anything that He can't supply. Is it knowledge? Is it strength? God can do more through a weakling who is yielded and trusting than He can through a strong man who isn't. "For all the promises of God in Him are yea, and in Him Amen, unto the glory of God by us" (2 Cor. 1:20, KJV).

I want the fellows and girls to whom I minister always to go away with this thought securely in their minds: "God, I'll never come to the place where I'm going to let the lack of anything persuade me that You are being hindered." I would rather you would go away with that in your hearts than with methods or materials or ideas that we may have to share with you, because I know the potential of the man who will come to the place where he can say hour after hour, day after day, week after week, month after month and year after year, "Lord, I believe my God reigneth."

Listen! You have an excuse if you want one. You have more than an excuse; you have hundreds of them. That isn't what's holding us back. It's that we don't live and preach the fact that He is on the throne. And when He's running the show, He will take care of all the props, even the transportation.

I was in Hong Kong on my way to India in 1948 when a Pan American flight was delayed long enough to make me miss my connection in Bangkok. I inquired if there were any way for me to get to Calcutta. The crew said, "No, not a chance in the world." Then one said, "We do have orders for this plane to go on to Calcutta, but because of regulations this crew can't take it." So I prayed, "Lord, You know about the meetings in Calcutta, and it's nothing for You to work this out."

We got to Bangkok and a radio message came, "We do not have a crew to bring this ship to Calcutta. Your crew ordered to bring it." Only four people were on that big DC-6, and the other three didn't have to go to India for three days. I arrived in time for those meetings, and as a result a man from Nepal came to know the Lord, a man who later became a key for getting the Gospel to that closed country way up in the Himalayas.

The need of the hour, as far as I'm concerned, is to believe that God is God, and that He is a lot more interested in getting this job done than you and I are. Therefore, if He is more interested in getting the job done, has all power to do it, and has commissioned us to do it, our business is to obey Him . . . reaching the world for Him and trusting Him to help us do it.

The Lord could easily have said to the disciples, "You fellows are only eleven men, and you lack facilities and transportation, so all I want you to do is start the fire in Jerusalem." But He didn't say that. The believers in South India testify they are glad Thomas believed Jesus Christ that he was to go to the uttermost part of the earth. I understand that the Mar Thoma Church, the largest in southern India, traces its origin back nineteen hundred years to the work of this disciple. Aren't you glad that Thomas didn't say to Jesus Christ, "I don't have a DC-6 yet"?

"Ye shall be witnesses unto Me in . . ." not *either* Jerusalem *or* Samaria *or* Judea *or* on the foreign field. You are to be witnesses, when you have the Holy Ghost, *"both* in Jerusalem, *and* in all Judea, *and* in Samaria, *and* unto the uttermost part of the earth."

Suppose you are a pastor. You have a responsibility to your people to be a shepherd to the flock. You also have a responsibility for people in other countries. You have to be concerned. The only reason you are not out there telling them about Jesus Christ is because you're training the lay people to love and serve the Lord Jesus Christ in your city, your state, and unto the uttermost part of the earth.

I used to have a map of the world that I kept before me. I'd put my fingers on some of the islands—Australia, New Zealand, Okinawa, Formosa—and say, "Lord, let me win men for You in these places." I wasn't challenged to do this by hearing a sermon, but by a verse of Scripture, Jeremiah 33:3, "Call unto Me, and I will answer thee, and shew thee great and mighty things, which thou knowest not." In the previous chapter Jeremiah had said to the Lord, "Ah Lord God! behold, Thou hast made the heaven and the earth by Thy great power and stretched out arm, and there is nothing too hard for Thee." Ten verses later the Lord says to Jeremiah, "I am the Lord, the God of all flesh: is there any thing too hard for Me?" Then just a few verses later He says, "All right, if you believe Me, call unto Me and I will answer."

I asked a buddy, "Do you believe this verse?" He said, "Yes." I said, "I do, too, but I've never seen these great and mighty things, and I'd like to." So we started a prayer meeting every morning. We decided to meet at a certain spot, have a fire built, and be in prayer by five o'clock. Not one minute after five . . . we just made it a date. We prayed two hours on weekdays but met at four on Sundays to pray for our Sunday school boys by name and for the Sunday school. We prayed for Harbor City, Torrance, Long Beach, San Pedro, Los Angeles, Pasadena, and the surrounding cities from which I had received calls from young Christian fellows saying, "Come over here and show us how you're reaching these boys."

The third and fourth weeks we started to include cities up the coast—San Francisco, Oakland, Seattle, and Portland. We said, "Lord, use us in these cities." By the fourth or fifth week we had covered every state in the Union. As we listed them we prayed, "Lord, use us to win young men to You in the State of Oregon. Use us to win young men in Massachusetts." Every morning we prayed for every one of the forty-eight states. Then about the sixth week one of us said to the other something like this: "If we believe God is big enough to let us win men in every one of the forty-eight states, let's go all out!"

We bought a world map and left it up in the Palos Verdes hills. Each morning we'd pull this old map out and pray that the Lord would use us in China and in Japan and in Korea. At the end of forty-two days I felt a burden lift. We stopped asking God to use us and began thanking Him that He was going to do so. "Now faith is the substance of things hoped for," and substance is substance. It's reality; it's something you can believe in. Faith comes by hearing, and hearing by the Word of God. We claimed the promises as we prayed. These promises were the brick and prayer was the mortar that put them together.

After forty-two days we discontinued our prayer meeting.

Three or four years later I was rummaging around in a drawer of the living room table when I found a little purple card—"Washington, Oregon." In another drawer was a list of names—Les Spencer from Illinois, John Dedrick of Texas, Gurney Harris from Arkansas, Ed Goodrick of Wisconsin. I discovered that men from every one of the forty-eight states had come to the Savior during those three or four years. God had answered, and these men were being trained as disciples. Then I thought of the world. "Why, Lord, am I permitted to have a part in this?" For the same reason you are.

"All power in heaven and earth is Mine. It's Mine for you to appropriate." This is not only a privilege; it's an order. He wants nothing less. God doesn't want you to take an island . . . He wants you to take the world. For what are you asking God? What do you want? Do you want to win a few? You'll have to start with the few, and you'll have to be successful with the few. You *can* be because Jesus said, "Follow Me, and I will make you fishers of men." No man ever followed Jesus who didn't become a fisher of men. He never fails to do what He promised. If you're not fishing, you're not following. You have to win one before you can win five, and five before you can win five hundred. The world is before you. How big is your faith?

The need of the hour is men who want what Jesus Christ wants and believe He wants to give them the power to do what He has asked. Nothing in the world can stop those men. Do you believe that? Do you want to be one of them? You may, but you will have to ask. "Call unto Me, and I will answer thee, and shew thee great and mighty things, which thou knowest not." Years ago when I prayed for Formosa I couldn't have comprehended what I'm seeing now. But that's the way He has promised it will be, so when you call, ask big!

Epilog and Reading List

In light of two thousand years of church history, the discipleship movement today is very young and its literature as yet is not plentiful. This anthology has attempted to integrate and unify what a few writers have written, and arrange their work in such a way that the reader will not only be challenged to be a disciple and become a disciple maker, but will have been given some tools and resources by which to begin this kind of ministry.

At its heart this is a ministry of copying—doing what Jesus Christ did and following His plan in terms of how He did it. The suggestions made by these writers hinge on our being convinced that this indeed was Jesus' master plan. If we are convinced, however, then we will seek out the specific methodology or develop our own. The main point is not merely to read and then say, "This is a nice book," but to take these principles and start practicing what they teach.

A practical suggestion is for you to go to a Christian Discipleship Seminar, led by Billie Hanks, and then apply the methodology learned to your own ministry. Next best is for you to familiarize yourself with the available literature, read it carefully, then develop your own program. To help you in this regard, the following reading list is given as a suggested starting point:

Coleman, Robert E. *The Master Plan of Evangelism*. Revell, 1963.

Cosgrove, Francis M., Jr. *Essentials of Discipleship*. NavPress, 1980.

Cosgrove, Francis M., Jr. *Essentials of New Life*. NavPress, 1978.

Eims, LeRoy. *Be the Leader You Were Meant to Be*. Victor, 1975.

Eims, LeRoy. *Disciples in Action*. NavPress, 1981.

Eims, LeRoy. *The Lost Art of Disciple Making*. Zondervan, 1978.

Eims, LeRoy. *What Every Christian Should Know About Growing*. Victor, 1976.

Hanks, Billie, Jr. *Everyday Evangelism*. Zondervan, 1981.

Hanks, Billie, Jr. *My Spiritual Notebook*. Word, 1977.

Henrichsen, Walter A. *Disciples Are Made—Not Born*. Victor, 1974.

Henrichsen, Walter A. *Discipling Your Family*. Victor, 1981.

Kuhne, Gary W. *The Dynamics of Discipleship Training*. Zondervan, 1978.

Kuhne, Gary W. *The Dynamics of Personal Follow-up*. Zondervan, 1977.

MacDonald, William. *True Discipleship* (Booklet). Walterick Publishers, 1962.

Moore, Waylon B. *New Testament Follow-up*. Eerdmans, 1963, 1970.

Sanny, Lorne C. *Marks of a Disciple* (Booklet). NavPress, 1975.

Trotman, Dawson E. *Born to Reproduce* (Booklet). NavPress, 1975.

Wilson, Carl. *With Christ in the School of Disciple Building*. Zondervan, 1976.